HEREDIA

by

W. N. INCE

THE ATHLONE PRESS

1979

Published by
THE ATHLONE PRESS
at 4 Gower Street, London WC1

Distributed by
Tiptree Book Services Ltd
Tiptree, Essex

U.S.A. and Canada
Humanities Press Inc
New Jersey

British Library Cataloguing in Publication Data
Ince, Walter Newcombe
  Heredia.—(Athlone French poets).
  1. Heredia, José-Maria de—Criticism and
  interpretation
  841'.8   PQ2275.H3Z/
  ISBN 0 485 14607 x cloth
  ISBN 0 485 12207 3 paperback

Printed in Great Britain by
Western Printing Services Limited
Bristol

Athlone French Poets

HEREDIA

Athlone French Poets

General Editor EILEEN LE BRETON
Reader in French Language and Literature,
Bedford College, University of London

Monographs

GERARD DE NERVAL
THEOPHILE GAUTIER
HEREDIA
VERLAINE
RIMBAUD
JULES LAFORGUE
PAUL VALERY
GUILLAUME APOLLINAIRE
SAINT-JOHN PERSE
FRANCIS PONGE
HENRI MICHAUX

Critical Editions

VICTOR HUGO : CHATIMENTS
GERARD DE NERVAL : LES CHIMERES
ALFRED DE MUSSET : CONTES D'ESPAGNE ET D'ITALIE
THEOPHILE GAUTIER : POESIES
JOSE-MARIA DE HEREDIA : LES TROPHEES
PAUL VERLAINE : SAGESSE
PAUL VERLAINE : ROMANCES SANS PAROLES
ARTHUR RIMBAUD : LES ILLUMINATIONS
JULES LAFORGUE : LES COMPLAINTES
PAUL VALERY : CHARMES OU POEMES
GUILLAUME APOLLINAIRE : ALCOOLS
SAINT-JOHN PERSE: EXIL
PONGE: LE PARTI PRIS DES CHOSES
MICHAUX : AU PAYS DE LA MAGIE

Athlone French Poets

General Editor EILEEN LE BRETON

This series is designed to provide students and general readers both with Monographs on important nineteenth- and twentieth-century French poets and Critical Editions of one or more representative works by these poets.

The Monographs aim at presenting the essential biographical facts while placing the poet in his social and intellectual context. They contain a detailed analysis of his poetical works and, where appropriate, a brief account of his other writings. His literary reputation is examined and his contribution to the development of French poetry is assessed, as is also his impact on other literatures. A selection of critical views and a bibliography are appended.

The Critical Editions contain a substantial introduction aimed at presenting each work against its historical background as well as studying its genre, structure, themes, style, etc. and highlighting its relevance for today. The text normally given is the complete text of the original edition. It is followed by full commentaries on the poems and annotation of the text, including variant readings when these are of real significance.

E. Le B.

CONTENTS

To Leslie
who helped me to think about
how to write

I

JOSE-MARIA DE HEREDIA

José-Maria de Heredia[1] was born in Cuba, that is, in Spanish territory, on 22 November 1842. His father, Don Domingo de Heredia, was Spanish and descended from a heroic lineage. The most impressive progenitor was undoubtedly Juan Fernando de Heredia, born at the beginning of the fourteenth century of one of the noblest families in Aragon, in southern Spain. The exploits of this brave, energetic and resourceful forbear were of massively epic proportions: negotiator for the papal court at Avignon, the pope's mediator in 1346 between the kings of France and England, fighting on the French side at the battle of Crécy-en-Ponthieu and then helping to conclude a truce, minister and friend of Pope Innocent VI, governor of Avignon and providing money for the construction of that famous city's huge walls, appointed in 1376 Grand Master of the Order of St. John of Malta and equipping an armada which Pope Gregory XI used to re-establish the papacy in Rome, fighting the Turks successfully in Patras but seized by them at Corinth, ransomed after three years of harsh captivity and mellowing into Christian humility and an extreme old age before being laid to his final rest in his native Aragon. It was in the sixteenth century that the first Heredia arrived in the Caribbean, Don Pedro de Heredia, one of the *conquistadores* in the expedition led by Bartholomew Columbus, Christopher Columbus's brother. Don Pedro had lost his nose battling in Italy and, at the head of his men, is reputed to have presented an awesome spectacle which quickly routed the natives. A heroic figure not much less epic than Juan Fernando, he founded the city of Cartagena de las Indias (now in Colombia), became governor of New Spain and after many adventures died in a shipwreck off the coast of Florida. In exchange for the rights he had relinquished as governor of Cartagena, Don Pedro was ceded a province on the island of Santo Domingo, Española or Hispaniola as it came to be known (it is now divided between Haiti on the western side of the island and the Dominican Republic on the east). In the latter part of the eighteenth century, the rich plantations of sugar-cane, coffee and cotton still belonged to the Heredia family; the poet's father, Don Domingo, was a collateral rather than a direct descendant of Don Pedro de Heredia.[2] The unrest and uprisings of the negroes and mulattos in the wake of the French Revolution at the end of the century caused the whites to flee the island. The Heredias were ruined by the revolt in Santo Domingo, led by the famous Haitian Toussaint Louverture: in 1801 they moved to the neighbouring island of Cuba, Don Domingo rebuilding his fortunes by creating fine coffee plantations—*la Fortuna, el Potosi*—on the mountainous eastern side of the island between Santiago and Guantánamo. The names of their three hundred slaves are set down in the family record book of Domingo and his wife.[3] By his first wife, Don Domingo had four children, a daughter and three sons. After her death, he married Louise Girard and had four more children, three daughters and a son, José-Maria, the last born.

These genealogical details are useful not only to help us to situate the origins and context of Heredia's early life but to understand how he will in later years see himself as belonging to a long and distinguished line; small wonder not just that he will compose a series of sonnets celebrating *Les Conquérants* (a sub-section of 'Le Moyen Age et la Renaissance' in *Les Trophées*) but that he will spend many years translating into carefully-wrought French the history in Spanish by Bernal Díaz of the discovery and conquest of New Spain by Cortés and his *conquistadores*.

Don Domingo's second wife and mother of the poet was French. Her great-grandfather, Girard d'Ouville, was in Louis XV's reign president of the Normandy *Parlement*. He had a son, godchild of Madame de Pompadour, who seems to have embodied a mettlesome pride worthy of the Heredia side of the poet's family: rejecting a brilliant marriage arranged by his father, he took the woman of his own choice, the daughter of a Dieppe shipmaster. Through the powerful influence of his godmother, he acquired the post of King's attorney in the island of Santo Domingo, married the young woman from Dieppe and moved to the Caribbean. By his mother's side of the family too, then, José-Maria had what used to be regarded as an ancestry of some distinction. Like the Heredias, the Girards left the island of

Santo Domingo after the native uprisings, settled in Cuba and, after great initial hardships, established rich coffee plantations there.

Reliable details, carefully interpreted, about the early years of any person can be invaluable for our understanding of basic character and disposition. Heredia was to remain in Cuba until September 1851, that is, until almost the age of nine but there is not much exact information available concerning these very first years. Ibrovac (see Bibliography) reads much into the sentimental, romanticized novel *Le Séducteur* by Heredia's daughter Marie (published in 1914 under her pen-name of Gérard d'Houville) and equates the child Panchito in that novel with Pepillo, as José-Maria de Heredia was known by all his family: Panchito-Pepillo is a Prince Charming in a fairy-tale, adored and spoiled by all from mother to humblest slave, courting at the tender age of nine the charming Silvana. But some firm assertions can be made. As a child, José-Maria was very happy, he enjoyed from birth the warm delights of an exotic island, he led an active physical life in the open air discovering tropical flowers and birds and acquiring a provision of images and memories that were to last him all his life. It was 'une enfance rêveuse, vaga-bonde, un peu sauvage'.[4] He accepted without question and enjoyed the comforts of his parents' relative wealth but above all, loving each other and their children, his parents gave Pepillo the reassuring background of a stable family life. Both parents, being intelligent and cultured, attached great importance to the proper instruction of their children, Heredia's mother particularly wanting him to be educated in France. He was encouraged to read: Lamartine, Hugo, Walter Scott, Goethe and the historian Barante were some of the writers he was to absorb. By good fortune, one of the close friends of Heredia's parents was Nicolas Fauvelle, a former planter who had re-turned to Senlis, a small town some twenty-seven miles north-east of Paris. Both Domingo and Louise de Heredia were well aware of the limited intellectual and cultural resources of the island of Cuba and they had no desire to see their child grow up to be an ignorant if prosperous creole. Soon after José-Maria's birth, Fauvelle offered to assume responsibility for the boy if he were brought up in France. Don Domingo's health began to fail in the later 1840s and on 15 April 1849 he died at sea just before the arrival in France of the ship that was taking him there for a recuperative holiday. Amid the grief of her bereavement and the increased responsibility she now felt for her children, Heredia's mother hesitated whether to have her son brought up in France or to send him to Spain with perhaps the later possibility of his following the diplomatic career of his elder step-brother Manuel, who eventually became governor of the Philippines. Events helped to decide the issue. Fauvelle's wife died in April 1850. During the widower's subsequent visit to Cuba the decision was taken that José-Maria should go back to France with him to enter, as a boarder, the collège Saint-Vincent de Senlis.

Many of the letters exchanged by Fauvelle and Madame de Heredia are still available and provide a very clear and objectively trustworthy source of information about the young boy and adolescent. Of particular interest are the reports which Fauvelle conscientiously sent to Cuba about the progress being made by his young charge. Heredia was undoubtedly lucky to have such a considerate guardian. Fauvelle was cautious and strongly conservative—in this respect, it seems, resembling the boy's parents. He was sometimes a little pompous by the standards of our own time and doubtless somewhat old-fashioned even in the middle of the nineteenth century. Writing to Madame de Heredia of the political situation in a letter of 12 February 1852, he reports that Louis Napoléon is now president: 'il a brisé l'assemblée et la tribune et réduit à néant la liberté de la presse'. Fauvelle is glad. 'Bénissons donc la Providence d'avoir substitué, à cette tour de Babel qu'on appelait l'assemblée législative, un homme énergique, à tête de fer, qui a su réprimer les factions, et rendre à l'autorité la considération et la force dont elle avait tant besoin'. In a letter of 26 July 1855 he moralizes concerning what he describes as the 'rigueur salutaire' exercised by the collège Saint-Vincent de Senlis, 'car j'attribue à l'excessive liberté, dont jouissent à Paris les écoliers et les étudiants, cette dissipation d'esprit, cette appétence de plaisirs ennemie de tout travail sérieux'. Given Fauvelle's traditionalist nature, the firm Catholic principles of the priests who taught at Saint-Vincent and the strict régime at the school, there was little risk of the young Heredia being ruined by excessive pampering; indeed, on 23

June 1857, Fauvelle tells Madame de Heredia that he will not let her son have as much pocket money as she suggests to avoid giving him 'les germes de l'orgueil'. But Fauvelle had a deep affection for Pepillo, who dined twice a week at his guardian's house in the suburb of Villevert, stayed there often during school holidays and reveals in his letters his fond respect for the man who showed him so much devotion and kindness. At times, Fauvelle was indulgent, at least he was aware with tolerant compassion that too much should not be expected of young children, as when in December 1857 he tells the mother not to pay too much attention to a school complaint of 'certaines habitudes de légèreté' (mainly, talking by José-Maria when he should have been silent) —'Comme si la légèreté n'était pas de son âge!'.

It is obvious from all sources that José-Maria was a naturally happy and active child: 'si le travail ne lui fait pas peur', Fauvelle reflects on 28 September 1854, 'il ne sait pas non plus ce que c'est que d'engendrer de la mélancolie, et de mal utiliser ses moments de loisir'. The address given by the mature Heredia in 1879[5] when he presided at the annual dinner of the school's old boys' association shows a traditionally tender, even sentimental, retrospection as he evokes the varied outdoor games the children in his time there played, some of their pursuits (like keeping silkworms in desks and rearing frogs) or their interesting archeological excursions in the surrounding countryside. From this affectionate man who enjoyed and returned the love of both his parents and, later, of his wife and three daughters, his most cogent memory comes in one sentence: 'Le collège a été pour nous tous une grande famille'. In the child and adolescent José-Maria there seems to have been little sustained introspection. His attention and energies were mostly directed to the world about him, his work and play at school, people and things. His nature was expansive, even exuberant. The talking out of turn in class to which reference has already been made was virtually the only criticism ever brought against his conduct at the school. There is a scene both touching and amusing recounted by Fauvelle (letter to Madame de Heredia in April 1853) when the school's term report arrives at his house. Pepillo was rather anxious about this report. In fact, his academic progress was described as excellent but, Fauvelle goes on with some humour,

il se permet quelquefois de bavarder à l'étude—et, dit le bulletin, c'est depuis quelques mois seulement qu'il est devenu causeur. Je soutiens, moi, que le bulletin n'est pas dans le vrai, car ce n'est pas depuis quelques mois, mais depuis qu'il est au monde, que Pepillo se permet d'avoir des idées et de les énoncer à l'aide de la parole.

The young José-Maria asks if his guardian will send the report to his mother because he fears it would grieve her. Vows are made—which were not entirely to be kept!—to avoid repetition of the offence and the report is thrown by Fauvelle into his study fire. It would be difficult to find better evidence than this letter of Pepillo's ready tongue, if not his garrulity, and of the tone of the relationship between the ten-year-old boy and the substitute father, the latter revealing part firmness, part affection carefully controlled so that he could later in his letter share with the mother his amused sympathy with his charge's earnest concern. This and other incidents described in Fauvelle's letters make it clear that Pepillo was eminently dutiful and eager to please others and elders—his distant mother, Fauvelle, the staff at the school. And he transparently had what used to be called 'winning ways': within days of entering the school and after a very short period of tears and homesickness, Pepillo has so charmed two ladies visiting their sons at the school that they treat him as one of their own children, regaling him with good things to eat. By July 1857, when Pepillo is nearly fifteen, Fauvelle is pleased with his own clear and cautious assessment:

> Ce qui me donne plus de contentement encore, c'est de sentir grandir en moi la conviction que votre enfant ne sera pas seulement un garçon d'esprit, et d'intelligence, mais qu'il vaudra son père au point d'avoir des idées sérieuses. Il est né bon; il est reconnaissant; il sera essentiellement amical, mais pas au point de se laisser exploiter par ceux qui tenteraient de le circonvenir ou de le tromper.

Heredia's general academic record at the school was very good. He excelled in Latin and Greek but also won prizes and honourable mentions in history and French. His weakest subject by far was arithmetic. So well was he doing in 1856 that he jumped a class: instead of spending the summer vacation with relations in Béarn, he remains in Senlis with Fauvelle, studying hard and taking some private lessons.[6] In October 1857, Pepillo enters his *année de rhétorique*, that is, the sixth form, and in December of that year Fauvelle points out to Madame de Heredia how understandable it is that a fifteen-year-old should be a little more boyish than his class-mates, all of whom are at least eighteen: no wonder he is 'un peu plus causeur que ses camarades'! But the young scholar's life was not all study. In June 1858 he took the role of Josabeth in a school production of Racine's *Athalie*—not easy, Fauvelle notes, when your moustache is starting to grow. Despite his mentor's anxiety, Pepillo did well: 'il a fait preuve, comme acteur, d'une grande sensibilité et d'une convenance parfaite'. For his vacations, when he was not staying with Fauvelle, Pepillo had relations to visit in different parts of France, such as his two married aunts, his mother's sisters, one at Mont near Arthez, in the Basses-Pyrénées, the other in Béarn. In November 1858, he passed his *baccalauréat*. A letter from Fauvelle on 25 February 1859 defines the nature of the sixteen-year-old boy:

Au résumé, il est d'un caractère honnête et franc, mais de cette franchise qui ne va pas jusqu'à dire son dernier mot, quand un peu de circonspection est nécessaire. Chez lui, l'imagination domine, mais en laissant une large part au bon sens. Il a beaucoup d'assurance, mais cette assurance n'a rien qui blesse, parce qu'elle est dans sa nature et vient de la conscience de sa valeur personnelle, et non d'un sentiment de fatuité ou d'orgueil. [. . .] Il se recommande surtout par une qualité de cœur bien précieuse à mes yeux, celle de la reconnaissance.

But Fauvelle goes on to speak of Pepillo's 'grand désir de paraître, défaut commun à tous les jeune créoles, [qui] peut paralyser toute une partie de ce que nous sommes en droit d'attendre de la droiture de son caractère et de son intelligence, surtout s'il est appelé à vivre en France loin des yeux de sa mère.' On 26 March Fauvelle described Pepillo as 'd'une intelligence remarquable'. We may then conclude that the adolescent had received a sound basic education in the humanities, he was happy to follow in the steps of his elders—Fauvelle or his masters at school—, he was intelligent, sensitive, imaginative, eager, impetuous, confident, bubbling over with energy and rather too fond of showing off.

With all his warm approval, Fauvelle's reservations were noted by Madame de Heredia and later in 1858 she planned a visit to France. In fact, José-Maria arrived home in Cuba, at the plantation *le Potosi*, by 10 June 1859. His mother was moved to the depths of her being by what France had made of her son and her gratitude to Fauvelle knew no bounds. For all her powerful maternal tenderness, she was shrewd enough to note in her Pepillo 'la fougue de ses impressions qui m'effraient' (10 August 1859): he is 'tout feu, tout domination, il *veut, il fait ce qu'il veut*' (16 December 1859). He spent three months at the Potosi plantation renewing his acquaintance with the country, his relations and friends and with the Spanish language which he soon came to speak again with fluency. He toyed with the idea of studying law in Havana and, writing to Fauvelle on 2 August 1859, wondered about his future career, asking for Fauvelle's advice: 'Ecrivez-moi longuement, bien cher ami; n'oubliez pas les bons conseils, ils ne sont jamais de trop pour un jeune homme'. It would perhaps be unworthy to wonder whether any diplomatic flattery lies behind the *sagesse* of such a sentence. Pepillo seems to have been naturally respectful, submissive and grateful, generous-hearted and idealistic even for his young years. In September, he went to Havana to study philosophy and literature. Both he and his mother quickly abandoned any idea of his settling in Cuba as an *habitant* or planter. She feared that, leading such a life, he would be quickly transformed, like others she had seen, into 'un pacha grossier'. When he returned to her in July 1860, he was reading as eagerly as ever, in French and Spanish, discussing literature whenever he could. Before leaving for France, Madame de Heredia and her son paid last visits to various places and people. A letter from Heredia to Fauvelle on 29 October 1860 described his impressions during their last visit to the plantation at *la Fortuna* where he had been born nearly eighteen years before:

Nous voilà installés, maman et moi, dans la vieille case de la pauvre Fortune que j'ai trouvée bien triste et bien désolée. Ces grandes savanes où il n'y a d'autre végétation que l'éternel mango, et cet air de solitude et d'abandon, m'ont tristement impressionné. La maison est toujours comme vous l'avez connue, le jardin a été bien entretenu et j'y ai retrouvé avec bonheur tout au fond la tonnelle de jasmin où vous m'avez donné ces premières et paternelles leçons qui ne s'oublient pas [. . .] J'espère que vous ne pourrez douter de tout le bonheur qu'aura votre ancien élève et pupille, qui est et sera toujours votre fils le plus chéri et le plus obéissant, à vous embrasser, et à reprendre sous vos ordres sa bonne vie de travail dont, depuis un an, il a été un peu dés-accoutumé. Soyez bien assuré que vous ne trouverez pas en moi un jeune homme léger et volontaire, mais bien l'enfant et le collégien dociles que vous voulez bien regretter un peu dans vos lettres. C'est bien aimable à vous, mon meilleur ami, de trouver que je vous manque. Maman pourra vous dire combien de fois et avec quelle affection j'a regretté de ne plus vous avoir pour me conduire doucement et paternellement, comme vous saviez si bien le faire.

We note, if confirmation is required, the affection and gratitude of the young Heredia for the guardian who had manifestly completed a thorough and tender guardianship. The quite sincere, almost cajolingly submissive tone which we have already encountered must have been part of the early capacity Heredia revealed for pleasing others. What is perhaps just as interesting is the perspective given on 'la vieille case de la pauvre Fortune': long before his mature studies of the Greek and Latin classics and the composition of poems like 'L'Oubli' and 'Sur un marbre brisé', there is in the eighteen-year-old youth a resonance which anticipates his later fondness for fixing the passage of time and the bitter-sweet sadness of things embodied in *solitude* and *abandon*. José-Maria and his mother left Cuba in April 1861 and arrived in Bordeaux in early June. He was never to set foot in his native island again.

After his return from Cuba, his permanent home was to be in Paris. By 1861, some of the main lines of his character and temper-ament were fairly discernible but his intellectual and artistic formation was of course far from complete. He registered at the Sorbonne on 4 November 1861 to study law. He lived with his mother and found time to pay frequent visits to Senlis. Brittany became a favourite haunt in holidays. In August 1862 he was successful in the examinations at the end of his first year. These law studies suffered a set-back in the summer of 1863, when he failed the examination, but he was successful in June 1864 and received his diploma of *bachelier en droit*. But while still following the lectures in law at the university, he had in November 1862 begun his studies at the *Ecole Nationale des Chartes*. In the three years of work for this institution, 1862–5, Heredia clearly dis-tinguished himself, being classed in the examinations among the

first three or four candidates. It is true that he did not complete
the thesis required to obtain his diploma at the end of the course
but, not being of French nationality—he was not to be naturalised
until after his election to the Académie française in 1894—he
would not even with the diploma have been eligible for the posts,
for instance, as archivist or librarian, epigraphist or art historian,
normally opened up to those who held it. Though the uprisings
in Cuba in 1868 were to reduce the family fortune, Heredia was
wealthy enough not to need regular employment. His training at
the *Ecole des Chartes* was an important stage in his evolution. It
would be naïve to emulate some later writers, particularly
those *littérateurs* who had never set foot inside the *Ecole des Chartes*,
in their excessively reverential awe for the knowledge Heredia
acquired there, but there can be no doubt that the study of
manuscripts, coins and seals, of archaeology, archives and
libraries, of political, ecclesiastical and civil geography, of civil,
feudal and commercial law, in short, of all matters relevant to the
understanding of France up to the Revolution, and especially of
the Middle Ages, gave Heredia a background of detailed historical
knowledge and developed interests that were to inform many of
the sonnets that make up *Les Trophées*. It is also understandable
that the controlled composition of his sonnets owed something to
the systematic, methodical approach encouraged by three years
of study at the *Ecole des Chartes*. As regards his studies for the
degree in law at the university, Heredia did well in 1866 in the
examinations at the end of the first year, but he did not submit
himself to any more examinations there.

For our present purposes, Heredia's life from this point on is
mainly represented by his literary activity and his involvement in
the trends of his time. His interest in poetry had been stimulated
and fostered from an early age by his mother. It seems that he was
writing poems before he reached the age of eleven. The relatively
small number of poems extant from his years in Cuba are often
diffuse and reveal the influences of his reading, particularly of
Lamartine and Musset, but he was already drawn to compose
a few sonnets. Even before he returned to Cuba in 1859 and long
before meeting and knowing Leconte de Lisle so well, Heredia
had experienced the love and influence of the older man's poetry.
It was the very day in 1858 when he learned he had passed his

baccalauréat that he bought a copy of Leconte de Lisle's *Poésies complètes* (Poulet-Malassis et de Broise, 1858). He read them again and again on the ship returning to Cuba and during his stay on the island.[7] But he had also been reading other writers such as Hugo, Chateaubriand and Ronsard. In January 1862 Heredia joined *La Conférence La Bruyère*, a society founded in the Faculty of Law, in which he was now enrolled, to study and discuss literature, art and philosophy. Their meetings were clearly lively, even though the discussion of politics and religion was theoretically excluded. In the society's yearbook for 1861–2 Heredia published several of his earliest poems: 'Nuits d'été', 'Mars', 'Ballade sentimentale', 'Chanson', 'Coucher de soleil', 'La Mort d'Agamemnon', 'L'Héliotrope', of which the last two were in sonnet form, as was 'Mer montante', to be published in the society's yearbook for 1862–3. Significantly, only 'L'Héliotrope' and 'Mer montante' were signed by Heredia. Already, he was unwilling to acknowledge the looser structure of the other poems, which are certainly his but which reveal little of the particular genius he was soon to cultivate. Already, the sonnet was the verse-form he was most happy and proud to adopt. Already, influenced by Leconte de Lisle's poetic example, he was encountering poets in the meetings of *La Conférence La Bruyère*—Sully Prudhomme, Georges Lafenestre, Emmanuel des Essarts—who must have helped to confirm his readiness to undergo and promote the predominant influence of his poetic career, that of *Le Parnasse*.

Le Parnasse contemporain, recueil de vers nouveaux was not to make its first appearance until 1866 but the tastes and tendencies that were eventually to achieve prominence through that publication were taking shape many years earlier in various reviews and gatherings of poets. The first, and very short-lived, of these publications worth our notice was the *Revue fantaisiste*, begun in 1861 by Catulle Mendès. This enthusiastic poet of eighteen years was encouraged by older and greater poets like Gautier, Baudelaire and Banville; many of those who were to become *Parnassiens*, like Albert Glatigny, Sully Prudhomme or Louis Bouilhet, contributed poems to it. The *Revue française*, founded in 1861 by Adolphe Amat, eschewed politics and encouraged young writers eager to publish; some of its contributors were inherited from the defunct *Revue fantaisiste*, like Mendès himself and Glatigny, but there were others whose names became better known as the Parnassian movement was formed: Georges Lafenestre, Léon Dierx, Emmanuel des Essarts and Heredia himself, who published there in 1863 five sonnets—'Le Triomphe d'Iacchos', 'Pan', the diptych 'Le Lis' and 'Vœu'—which he later stigmatized as *libertins*, that is, irregular, and four of which he excluded from *Les Trophées* in 1893.[8] In 1864, it was the turn of the *Revue de Paris* to publish three of Heredia's sonnets, one new, 'La Mort de l'aigle', and two—'L'Héliotrope' and 'Mer montante'—which had already appeared, as has been noted, in the yearbooks of *La Conférence La Bruyère*. Other contributors were Gautier, Banville, Emmanuel des Essarts, Louis Bouilhet and Léon Cladel. Another publication of some importance in these early years was the *Revue du progrès*, founded in 1863 by Louis-Xavier de Ricard, which published, pseudonymously, Verlaine's first poems. Ricard and Mendès were leaders of a sort and entertained their young poet friends in their own homes and took them to each other's: Mendès received on Wednesdays, Ricard—or perhaps more properly, his mother, la marquise de Ricard—on Fridays. These meetings of enthusiastic young artists were lively, sometimes noisy, as they discussed and recited poetry, often intoxicated enough by their commitment to poetry to need no stronger drink than tea. Another salon, gayer still and more extravagant than those of Mendès and Ricard, was Nina de Villard's, where open table was kept for all comers and Madame Villard's musical talents were regularly required. But all these gatherings were eclipsed by the crucial, culminating reception of the week, on Saturdays, at Leconte de Lisle's small flat on the fifth floor at 8 Boulevard des Invalides. Up the narrow stairway that led to this sanctum there climbed many of the poets who were to be associated with the new poetic movement: Mendès, Banville, Ménard, Coppée, Villiers de l'Isle-Adam, Dierx, Silvestre, Prudhomme, Lafenestre and Heredia. Though the conversation could be animated in Leconte de Lisle's salon and the tone heated, not least when Leconte de Lisle himself was delivering some energetic diatribe, the young disciples regarded with unanimous veneration the Master who by the force of his example in his *Poèmes antiques* (1852) and *Poèmes barbares* (1862), as well as by the force of his teaching and presence in his salon, represented for them all a summit of poetic achievement. Of all these young poets, Heredia was to become by far the closest friend of the Master and perhaps the nearest to him in the artistic aims he was to embody in *Les Trophées*. In 1894, by then a member of the Académie française which he was representing at the funeral service of Leconte de Lisle, Heredia looked back over three decades of close friendship and collaboration to sum up the older poet's influence:

> Illustre avant d'être célèbre, il n'a pas cherché le succès, il a conquis la gloire. L'influence de son noble génie fut salutaire. Durant trente années il fut, pour les jeunes poètes, un éducateur, un modèle incomparable. Il avait l'âme tendre et fière, un esprit profond et charmant. Tous ceux qui l'ont connu, l'aimaient autant qu'ils le vénéraient. Il a été pour nous le vrai maître, un maître amical et fraternel.[9]

The events immediately preceding the appearance in 1866 of *Le Parnasse contemporain, recueil de vers nouveaux* are now as legendary as the formation of the *Pléiade* in the sixteenth century or, in the nineteenth, the triumph of Romantic drama at the *bataille d'Hernani*. Alphonse Lemerre was the owner of a bookshop at 47 passage Choiseul, whose principal clients were buyers of prayerbooks and other works suitable for pious people. Lemerre was thinking of bringing out an edition of the poets of the Pléiade when he was asked to publish the poems of Xavier de Ricard (*Ciel, rue et foyer*, 1865) and later of other young poets. In the early days, publication was at the poets' expense! Lemerre also took over the journal *L'Art* which had been started elsewhere by the same Xavier de Ricard. The young poets who had assembled in the premises where *L'Art* had been first published transferred themselves to Lemerre's bookshop in the passage Choiseul and they were joined there by others at what became, from 1865, regular daily meetings. The noise and long-haired appearance of these young men risked disturbing more sedate customers; Lemerre was led therefore to give his young poets a back-room on the mezzanine floor, reached by a spiral staircase. This was to be the much celebrated *Entresol du Parnasse*, an area sometimes so crowded that late-comers had to sit on the stairs, where from four to seven every afternoon the future Parnassians recited their own poems and others' and passionately discussed all aspects of poetry. The mood was serious and light-hearted by turns, usually good-tempered and sometimes uproarious. The memoirs written later in the century about these golden days of the 1860s often mention the ebullient presence of the young Heredia, impeccably dressed—unlike some of his companions—and usually very much to the fore and in the thick of discussion and activity. Many of the regular attenders at Lemerre's *entresol* were poets who also frequented the salons of Mendès, Ricard, Villard and Leconte de Lisle. Gabriel Marc's poem 'L'Entresol du Parnasse' became a much quoted evocation of the figures seen at Lemerre's, of whom the most notable were Dierx, Armand Renaud, Coppée, Glatigny, Sully Prudhomme, Henry Cazalis, Armand Silvestre, Mendès, Emmanuel des Essarts, Anatole France, Xavier de Ricard and Heredia. José-Maria's presence was well captured:

> Tout tremble: c'est Heredia
> A la voix farouche et vibrante,
> Qu'en vain Barbey parodia.[10]
> Tout tremble: c'est Heredia,
> Heredia qu'incendia
> Un rayon de mil huit cent trente![11]
> Tout tremble: c'est Heredia
> A la voix farouche et vibrante.
> *(Sonnets parisiens*, 1875)

Older members, with settled reputations, such as Leconte de Lisle, Gautier and Banville, also joined the young zealots.

The term *Parnassien* was not of course to be applied to these poets until 1866 and later; it was at first a rather derisive label, coined from the title, *Le Parnasse contemporain* (which seems to have owed its name to *Le Parnasse satyrique* of the seventeenth-century poet, Théophile de Viau), but it was soon adopted by the poets themselves. Some later denied that they formed a school or movement. *Groupe* was the most cohesive term that, for instance, Catulle Mendès would allow to describe them, in his *Légende du 'Parnasse contemporain'* (1884). At the Saturday meetings in his salon, Leconte de Lisle gave much advice that was respectfully absorbed and often observed by his neophytes; he heard and corrected poems that were submitted to his judgement. But there were no interdictions and there was no party line. Each Parnassian poet was free to develop his own talent and express what was unique to him. Thus Leconte de Lisle's own poetry usually has a philosophic background, a high seriousness and a contained impersonal strength of feeling which stamp it as quite different from the poetry of Théodore de Banville, equally enamoured of ancient Greece but mostly lighter in tone and more playfully experimental than that of the Master. What united this group of poets was a certain number of attitudes and tendencies. A new generation is often best defined by its opposition to its predecessors or at least by its differences. The poet who received the scantest respect from the Parnassians was Alfred de Musset (though not all despised him and Heredia himself respected his work). Musset and, to some extent, Lamartine represented for our poets an over-personalized, insipid, sentimental *vague à l'âme* which offended their desire for more objective, controlled and compact writing. The sonnet was to become a favoured verse-form because more than any other it aided and patently embodied this ideal. In his poem 'A Ronsard' (*Les Vignes folles*, 1860), the young Albert Glatigny spoke for many when he conveyed his disgust for the sentimental, formless poetry which had been produced by some Romantic poets and which, following the example of Musset and Lamartine, was still popular in the middle of the nineteenth century:

> Moi, que tout ce pathos ennuie
> A l'égal de la froide pluie,
> Je veux, rimeur aventureux,
> Lire encor, Muse inviolée,
> Quelque belle strophe étoilée
> Au rythme doux et savoureux;
>
> Un fier sonnet, rubis, topaze,
> Ciselé de même qu'un vase
> De Benvenuto Cellini.

Distaste for effusiveness or even for too directly personal revelation was allied with a rejection of what were thought to be the facile values of the man-in-the-street and of the contemporary society that could not appreciate good art in any form. The Latin poet Horace's theme of *odi profanum vulgus* was given its most proud and fiercely contemptuous expression by Leconte de Lisle in, significantly, a sonnet:

Tel qu'un morne animal, meurtri, plein de poussière,
La chaîne au cou, hurlant au chaud soleil d'été,
Promène qui voudra son cœur ensanglanté
Sur ton pavé cynique, ô plèbe carnassière!

Pour mettre un feu stérile en ton œil hébété,
Pour mendier ton rire ou ta pitié grossière,
Déchire qui voudra la robe de lumière
De la pudeur divine et de la volupté.

Dans mon orgueil muet, dans ma tombe sans gloire,
Dussé-je m'engloutir pour l'éternité noire,
Je ne te vendrai pas mon ivresse ou mon mal,

Je ne livrerai pas ma vie à tes huées,
Je ne danserai pas sur ton tréteau banal
Avec tes histrions et tes prostituées.
              'Les Montreurs' (*Poèmes antiques*, 1852)

The Parnassian poets were to achieve fame and good sales of their poems before the end of the 1860s but they were never truly popular, particularly in the early days of the decade, and they were proud to be in this position; it mirrored their ambition to purify their art, to give it the dignity and even isolation which, in their eyes, it necessarily entailed. 'L'idéal du vrai poète a été et sera toujours le contraire de celui du public', wrote Léon Dierx in the preface to his collection of poems *Les Lèvres closes* (1871).

The preoccupation of the Parnassians with what is vaguely called 'form' is a major factor for our understanding of them. Before the term *Parnassien* became consecrated by usage, other short-lived labels crystallized this aspect of their endeavours: as well as *impassibles* they were called *stylistes* and *formistes*. In negative terms, their concern for form is a reaction against what they saw as loose, careless, flabby writing by earlier poets. For the Parnassians, *forme* was not just a secondary consideration, a way of describing the means whereby a poet communicated the more important *fond* or ideas he had. Ideas as such were not the particular domain of poetry. Form was as important as content, form was indeed a part of content: the inseparability of *forme* and *fond* was their way of purifying poetry of its more prosaic elements. For them, the best poet was the subtle, conscious manipulator of language. So-called 'inspired' composition risked degenerating into flatulent, over-sincere prolixity. In practice, considerations of form for many Parnassians therefore involved the need for careful, ordered composition, French that was correct as well as being lyrical, good rhymes, preferably 'rich', and language that was both evocative and precise. The *mot juste* becomes both a kind of rallying-cry and a widespread practice—the practice never stronger than in Heredia himself. All these aspirations of Parnassian poetry are brilliantly summed up by the young Verlaine in the first flush of his enthusiasm for the ideals he shares (and which he will not fully exemplify even in his early poetry and will later quite abandon):

> Ah! l'Inspiration superbe et souveraine,
> L'Egérie aux regards lumineux et profonds,
> Le Genium commode et l'Erato soudaine,
> L'Ange des vieux tableaux avec des ors au fond [. . .]
>
> La Colombe, le Saint-Esprit, le saint délire,
> Les Troubles opportuns, les Transports complaisants,
> Gabriel et son luth, Apollon et sa lyre,
> Ah! l'Inspiration, on l'invoque à seize ans!
>
> Ce qu'il nous faut à nous, les Suprêmes Poètes
> Qui vénérons les Dieux et qui n'y croyons pas,
> A nous dont nul rayon n'auréola les têtes,
> Dont nulle Béatrix n'a dirigé les pas,
>
> A nous qui ciselons les mots comme des coupes
> Et qui faisons des vers émus très froidement,
> A nous qu'on ne voit point les soirs aller par groupes
> Harmonieux au bord des *lacs* et nous pâmant, [12]
>
> Ce qu'il nous faut, à nous, c'est, aux lueurs des lampes,
> La science conquise et le sommeil dompté,
> C'est le front dans les mains du vieux Faust des estampes,
> C'est l'Obstination et c'est la Volonté! [. . .]
>
> Libre à nos Inspirés, cœurs qu'une œillade enflamme,
> D'abandonner leur être aux vents comme un bouleau:
> Pauvres gens! l'Art n'est pas d'éparpiller son âme;
> Est-elle en marbre, ou non, la Vénus de Milo?

> Nous donc, sculptons avec le ciseau des Pensées
> Le bloc vierge du Beau, Paros immaculé,
> Et faisons-en surgir sous nos mains empressées
> Quelque pure statue au péplos étoilé [. . .]
>   (from 'Epilogue', in *Poèmes saturniens*, 1866)

But poets, even Parnassian poets, do not live by form alone, still less by pronouncements about it, however eloquent and well turned. If we look at the themes of the Parnassians' poems, we are struck by their fondness for all manifestations of beauty and particularly for pictorial effects as well as for those arts which make a predominantly visual appeal. Poets are repeatedly seen as emulating the painter or sculptor. The images used by Verlaine in the stanzas just quoted of the poet 'chiselling' and 'sculpting' words and ideas are typical and directly descended from Gautier's famous poem 'L'Art' in the 1858 edition of *Emaux et camées* where the peremptory injunction to the poet is

> Sculpte, lime, cisèle;
> Que ton rêve flottant
> Se scelle
> Dans le bloc résistant!

The *transposition d'art*—expression of one art's aims or ideals in the medium of another—was the most striking representation of this aesthetic ideal and most successfully exploited by Gautier and Heredia. The Parnassian poets tend in their poetry to turn away from contemporary society, disgusted by its ugliness and stupid materialism, disheartened by its naïve, muddled and self-seeking politics. Many turn to the past, to an imagined age, especially that of classical Greece, when beauty and harmony were duly honoured by both artists and society. Leconte de Lisle's *Poèmes antiques* (1852) gave powerful impetus to this tendency, but, though the most important, Leconte de Lisle was only one of many.

I have suggested that the Parnassians can perhaps be best understood, at least initially, in the light of their opposition to certain Romantic poets such as Musset and Lamartine and to those poets—and they were legion—who wrote in their manner without their genius. But no creation comes *ex nihilo*, poetic or other, and the Parnassians can just as cogently be seen as continuing and extending the example set by other Romantic poets, since the term Romanticism covers diverse poets and emphases. To some extent, Hugo influenced every poet in the nineteenth century, if only by his liberating example in the field of vocabulary, rhythm and versification. The Hugo who was to influence the Parnassians was not the humanitarian idealist and visionary but the author of *Les Orientales* (1829), those vivid verbal pictures of the languor and implicit ferocity of the East in poems that were in the 1830s to be a dazzling revelation to poets then young, like Leconte de Lisle, for their striking imagery and rhythms—author, too, of the first series of *La Légende des siècles* (1859), epic scenes from man's spiritual and historical evolution. Théophile Gautier, 'le bon Théo', was to die in 1872 but however diminished by the 1860s in terms of his personal presence, he attended the meetings of the young Parnassians and encouraged their efforts; his past writings both as poet, above all in *Emaux et camées* (1852), and as prose-writer and theorist of *l'art pour l'art* which he propounded in the 1830s—cf. his seminal preface to his novel *Mademoiselle de Maupin* (1835)—formed a direct link with the principles and practice of the new poets. Gautier was a bridge between Romanticism and *Le Parnasse*. In 1856, in *L'Artiste*,[13] Gautier is enunciating ideas that recall the preface to *Mademoiselle de Maupin*. They are Parnassian *avant la lettre* and very much foreshadow what Heredia will accomplish in many sonnets:

> Après avoir vu, notre plus grand plaisir a été de transporter dans notre art à nous nos monuments, fresques, tableaux, statues, bas-reliefs, au risque souvent de forcer la langue et de changer le dictionnaire en palette [. . .] L'art pour nous n'est pas le moyen, mais le but [. . .] Une belle forme est une belle idée, car que serait-ce qu'une belle forme qui n'exprimerait rien.

Before the end of the 1840s there had begun a strong revival of Hellenic and Roman values in both the theatre and poetry, of which noteworthy examples were: Edgar Quinet's verse drama *Prométhée* (1838), Ponsard's classical tragedy *Lucrèce* (1843) and his short comedy *Horace et Lydie* (1850), Augier's plays *La Ciguë* (1844) and *Le Joueur de flûte* (1845), the prose poem by Maurice de Guérin *Le Centaure* (1840) and Victor de Laprade's narrative poem *Psyché* (1841). Théodore de Banville's poems *Les Cariatides*

(1842) helped to diffuse the Grecian ideal that was to be more magnificently displayed in Leconte de Lisle's *Poèmes antiques* (1852). And behind the work of poets and writers lay the philosophic, historical, archaeological and other scientific researches into the past that would cause Hippolye Taine, for example, and, later, Paul Bourget, to celebrate the marriage of science and art. The immediate predecessors in poetry or theatre exemplified traits that were in some degree to be characteristic of all the Parnassians: impersonality, compact, well-planned composition, correctness if not perfection of form, exoticism, return to much earlier or classical times and a general fusion of art and historical interest.

Such, in brief outline, was the background and context for all the poets who assembled in the *Entresol du Parnasse* at Lemerre's bookshop. The first *livraison* of the *Parnasse contemporain* appeared on 3 March 1866. Seventeen more instalments were to appear between then and June. Later in 1866 the eighteen instalments were published together in book form. The direction of the enterprise was in the hands of Catulle Mendès and Xavier de Ricard, and this included decisions concerning the contributors, of whom there were thirty-seven, ranging from the older Gautier, Banville, Leconte de Lisle and Baudelaire to some twenty relatively young poets like Verlaine, Mallarmé, Coppée and, with several sonnets, Heredia. A measure of Heredia's growing stature was that he served on the committee in charge of the second *Parnasse contemporain*, due to appear in 1869 but, owing to the Franco-Prussian war, not published until 1871; it was here that Heredia published the epic poem that was to be included in the edition of *Les Trophées* in 1893: 'La Détresse d'Atahuallpa. Prologue: Les Conquérants de l'or.' This prologue was as far as he got. The full poem was never completed. Heredia also served on the committee responsible for the third and last *Parnasse contemporain* of 1876, in which he published twenty-five 'sonnets héroïques'. The decade between the first and third *Parnasse contemporain* thus saw the emergence of Heredia as a leading Parnassian poet and a recognized master of the sonnet form, and of sonnets that by theme and style, with all the influences that were at work on him, bore his individual mark.

In February 1867 Heredia married Louise Despaigne. They

were to have three children, all daughters: Hélène (1871–1952), who married Maurice Maindron in 1899 and whose second husband was René Doumic; Marie (1875–1963), who married the poet Henri de Régnier in 1895 and who, as Gérard d'Houville, achieved some fame as a poet and writer; Louise (1877–1930) who married the poet and novelist Pierre Louÿs in 1898 and whose second husband was the comte Gilbert de Voisins. Since much of the correspondence between Heredia, his wife and their children will not be available for consultation until 1986, it is not possible to gain a detailed knowledge of their relationships, but those older letters that are available, including some written by Heredia to his mother in the early years of his marriage (his mother died in 1877), give glimpses of a happy and united family and of a father who doted on his young children. 'Elle est de plus en plus gentille quoique d'une vivacité endiablée,' Heredia writes to his mother on 8 April 1872 of his first-born, Hélène. 'Elle m'aime bien, m'embrasse avec joie et me baise respectueusement la main, à la mode espagnole [. . .] Si tu l'entendais rire aux éclats quand je la prends dans mes bras pour lui faire danser la polka ou la valse, tu en raffolerais'. Hélène clearly inherited the liveliness of her father noted by his own mother when he was a child, so much so that on one occasion Hélène caught her father's eye with one of her finger-nails, giving him a few painful and anxious days. The tender father's eye quickly recovered but, with a charming touch of domestic intimacy, he reassured his mother, 'l'expérience m'a rendu prudent et malgré tout le plaisir que j'ai à la voir faire ses diableries sur ma tête et ma barbe, je ferme avec soin les yeux'. We can be sure that Marie was no less lively and it is evident that Heredia's daughters loved him deeply.[14] Marie's literary bent declared itself early: at the age of seven this child was submitting her little prose poems to the great Leconte de Lisle, whose sombre moods were often lightened by his close contact with the affectionate, cheerful atmosphere of his younger friend's family.[15] At his home on Thursday evenings, Heredia entertained friends whose names are nearly all associated with *Le Parnasse*—Leconte de Lisle, of course, Coppée, Prudhomme, Lafenestre, Anatole France or Bourget. He was a visitor at the homes or receptions of other notable Parnassians or Parnassian sympathizers, such as Gautier, Banville and Flaubert.[16]

The period from his marriage to the publication of *Les Trophées* in 1893 witnessed the gradual growth of Heredia's reputation as he published his sonnets in collections and periodicals. The collections of sonnets were all issued by Lemerre: *Sonnets et eaux-fortes* (1868), three *Livre des sonnets* (1874, 1875, 1893), the four volumes of the *Anthologie des poètes français du XIXe siècle* (1887–8). The periodicals in which Heredia published were many and varied: *L'Artiste*, *La Revue des lettres et des arts*, *La Renaissance littéraire et artistique*, *La Revue du monde nouveau, littéraire, artistique, scientifique*, *La République des lettres*, *Le Monde poétique*, *Les Lettres et les arts*, *La Vie moderne* and, final achievement, *La Revue des deux mondes*. The translation of the *Véridique Histoire de la conquête de la Nouvelle Espagne* from the original Spanish of Bernal Díaz, in four volumes which were published by Lemerre in 1877, 1879, 1881 and 1887, was a labour of love that took Heredia many years and received two prizes from the Académie française: the four volumes run to over 1600 pages. The publication, either individually or in very small numbers, of Heredia's sonnets in periodicals and books was reinforced by his own recitations in salons and gatherings of artists and *mondains*. Over this period of more than twenty years, it became fashionable in society, even a trifle snobbish, to be able to recite the latest Heredia sonnet. In Jules Lemaître's famous phrase, Heredia was 'à la fois presque inédit et presque célèbre!'

His receptions on Saturday at his home in the Rue Balzac, from 1885, marked a high point of influence: those who attended included older Parnassians like Leconte de Lisle, who was to die in 1894, André Theuriet, Henry Cazalis and Sully Prudhomme but also many younger poets like Henri de Régnier, Pierre Louÿs and Paul Valéry. Heredia's friends were not confined to the literary world. Several, for instance, were concerned with art and craftsmanship, like Claudius Popelin,[17] painter, restorer and enameller, Edmond Bonnaffé, erudite collector of period furniture, Charles Yriarte and Edouard de Beaumont who were interested in swords and armorial bearings, or Charles Davillier, who enthusiastically garnered *objets d'art*. Others who attended were the painter Jules Breton, Henry Bordeaux, le vicomte de Guerne, Maurice Maindron, Emile Pouvillon and Edmond Biré. Though he went to others' salons—Daudet's, Taine's,

Edmond de Goncourt's, for example—Heredia preferred to receive in his own home. This he did with a quite individual combination of exuberance and civility. The accounts of his salon[18] are unanimous in their praise of the host. Heredia's appearance was almost as striking as it had been during the 1860s in the *Entresol du Parnasse*, with his flowing hair and beard, his slightly swarthy complexion, his firm, confident, posture with shoulders thrown back, his direct glance, his ringing voice, his curious stammer which became an added attraction for those who knew him, especially when he read poems[19], the exceedingly affable manner with which he welcomed his guests, offering cigars and tobacco, the way he moved from group to group discussing freely and loudly as he smoked his cigar or stuffed his pipe which needed regular relighting because its owner was so busy talking. His comments were as direct and frank as his glance. He welcomed all with the same enthusiastic cordiality and was always ready to perform a service—to give an introduction, a piece of advice—especially for the young and needy. With an appropriate audience he was very fond of comic anecdotes: 'Est-ce drôle!', it seems, was a refrain in his company. The animated young Pepillo was very present in the mature man of letters.[20]

The publication of *Les Trophées* in 1893 was partly in response to repeated requests from those who wanted to enjoy all his sonnets in an easily available form. It marked the zenith of Heredia's career. The public's reaction was strongly favourable (see Chapters IV and VI), the sales impressively high and quick. With remarkable speed he was the next year elected to the Académie française and, exceptionally, at the first round of voting. He deserved his honour but being well-known in fashionable and influential circles undoubtedly helped him; after all, his fame rested on no more than a book of sonnets and his translation of Bernal Díaz.[21] He was preferred to Verlaine and Zola. The great poet and novelist did not find favour with all because of what was seen as the vulgarity, not to say salacity, of some of their writings by the many sedate, conservative occupants of the forty *fauteuils* of the Académie française. Verlaine, who, with his astute aesthetic discrimination, always appreciated Heredia's worth as a poet, had the compensation of being elected *Prince des poètes* by the *Congrès des poètes*, with seventy-seven votes; Heredia came second, with thirty-eight votes. He took his seat in the Académie française in 1895. In 1896 he was appointed literary director of *Le Journal*: he chaired the newspaper's literary competitions and conscientiously selected the winners but seems to have been disillusioned by the little importance accorded to his work by his employers. In 1901 he was the correspondent for the Buenos Aires newspaper *El País*. In 1901, too, there began the last stage in Heredia's life, when he was put in charge of the Bibliothèque de l'Arsenal, that cradle of Romanticism early in the century under the direction of Charles Nodier. This new responsibility was eminently suited to the talents of our *ancien chartiste*, who threw himself with zeal into various tasks, the library's restoration, the purchase of manuscripts, the care and display of its precious books which he, as much as anyone, appreciated with a rare passion. The Saturday receptions at the Rue Balzac became the Arsenal's Sundays, presided over by an affable poet whose health was failing through the diabetes from which, it seems, he may have suffered.[22] One notes in his correspondence the number of times he was subject to various indispositions or took the waters at different spas. His eyes gave him trouble as early as the 1870s, he was suffering from gout in 1877, his hearing was affected before he took over at the Bibliothèque de l'Arsenal. Various anecdotes, mostly humorous ones from him, testify to the strict diet he had to follow in his last years as he grew weaker. The last months of his life were spent at the invitation of friends amid the rural calm of the castle of Bourdonné in Condé-sur-Vesgres where he died on 2 October 1905.

It seems that few readers of *Les Trophées*, even those who love and know them well, have much idea of the kind of person their author was, mainly because these famous sonnets are devoid of direct, personal self-revelation. If we had to conjecture, many of us, like Antoine Albalat,[23] would assume Heredia was reserved and formal. In his relations with others, the evidence we have— and it runs from the time of the young Pepillo to that of the mature academician—demonstrates that his nature, as experienced and seen by his contemporaries, was exactly contrary to the one assumed. Many descriptions by friends and acquaintances confirm the impression gained from letters that he was all expansiveness and exuberant vitality. But it would be another mistake to see his manner with others as unctuous back-slapping. Several witnesses confirm that he somehow combined familiarity with distinction: Coppée explains with a neat turn of phrase that in Heredia 's'alliaient, le plus naturellement du monde, un gentilhomme accompli et un bon garçon', writing of 'la libre, mais toujours correcte élégance de [sa] personne',[24] while Barrès captures the same qualities when he describes him welcoming his guests 'd'un geste large et d'une voix retentissante, avec une magnificence mêlée de bonhomie'.[25] Yet another error would be to conclude that Heredia was simply a complacent extrovert. Extrovert he certainly was, in so far as that term denotes the vague idea of energies directed towards the outside world, but Heredia's nature needs much more careful definition: the poet Henri de Régnier, who must have had ample time to study his father-in-law, saw him as 'une figure très complexe en son apparente simplicité'.[26] While not seeking to emulate the generally deterministic assumptions of a Sainte-Beuve or of Heredia's friend and admirer Hippolyte Taine, we would do well to bear in mind the following considerations.

In the first place, like Théophile Gautier, Heredia was very much 'un homme pour qui le monde extérieur existe'. His interests encompassed plants, trees and birds, all aspects of nature as much as of man and the history of man (cf. Ibrovac, i. p. 195); he was captivated by the richness and variety of all life. His detailed knowledge of facts and terms is linked with his love of *le mot juste* and also of the picturesque and exotic. It will become clear when we look at his sonnets and his views on poetry that he had no intimations of Sartrian, twentieth-century views concerning the malleability of man; he conservatively accepted the notion of an unchanging human nature. Antoine Albalat recounts some amusing anecdotes that can help us to understand Heredia's viewpoint, as when he said of the contemporary poet Moréas: ' "C'est un charmant garçon. Je l'aime beaucoup. Il a fait quelques beaux vers". Il ajouta, après une pause, comme une simple constatation: "J'ai rarement vu un cerveau aussi nul. Il ne sait absolument rien, et n'a guère lu que les poètes du seizième siècle" ', or when, after a certain visitor had just sent in his card: ' "Faites-le entrer", dit le maître, et, se tournant vers nous d'un air confidentiel: "'C'est un tel . . . Un excellent homme, très bon garçon . . . Un raseur effrené . . ." '.[27] In such remarks there is doubtless a measure of patronising condescension on Heredia's part, perhaps some superficiality and certainly some indiscretion[28] but no malice, I think, rather, evidence of his sometimes devastatingly frank appraisal of the curious combination of traits he encounters in some people, a kind of phenomenological fascination with the specificity of what is, at least for him, simply given. His frequent 'Est-ce drôle!' can be interpreted in the same way, as the intrigued observer's bemused response to experience. Heredia was all the more inclined to appreciate his fellow-men from this viewpoint because it entailed for him no validation, overt or covert, of his own worth. His own values were not in question: he took for granted his own estimate of himself. Fauvelle had remarked of the sixteen-year-old Pepillo that 'il a beaucoup d'assurance, mais cette assurance n'a rien qui blesse, parce qu'elle est dans sa nature et vient de la conscience de sa valeur personnelle, et non d'un sentiment de fatuité ou d'orgueil' and this shrewd appraisal is almost exactly repeated over fifty years later by Léon Barracand, writing of Heredia at the height of his career.[29] With such an assured or self-assured psychological basis, Heredia gave himself the more whole-heartedly to his enjoyment of the world about him. I think this is partly what Gabriel Hanotaux meant when he said Heredia 'avait l'âme d'un enfant'.[30]

The justification for my present remarks, and indeed for many about Heredia in this chapter, is that it is perhaps interesting and worthwhile in itself to discover more about a man so little known and to explain how he appeared to others in his day and, as far as we can assess, how he appeared to himself. If such a documentary value is granted, one may well wonder whether the picture of Heredia that emerges will help us in any way to understand and appreciate his poetry. I believe it can, despite the dangers so cogently stigmatized by a Proust or a Valéry of conclusions based on a naïvely biographical or clumsily deterministic approach. 'Un livre est le produit d'un autre moi que celui que nous manifestons dans nos habitudes, dans la société, dans nos vices', wrote Marcel Proust. 'Ce moi-là, si nous voulons essayer de le comprendre, c'est au fond de nous-même, en essayant de le recréer en nous, que nous pouvons y parvenir'[31]. As we read the sonnets and make them live in ourselves, we shall need to make this effort of imagination, but we can perhaps control and inform it a little more than some of the most recent of French critics who, however brilliant, have sometimes soared beyond Proust and Valéry into a private world of autonomous values. Heredia was intelligent and very cultured but not an intellectual as many since the Second World War would understand the concept. He was not given to intense metaphysical speculation, either in his life or in his poetry. Politics bored him: his remarks on this subject in his letters are dismissively contemptuous[32]. Ideas as such were not a Parnassian poet's concern. Introspection was not his natural bent. By some modern criteria, of course, he was a reactionary, bourgeois conservative and a moral and metaphysical coward precisely because he did not ask himself enough questions; his luxurious aesthetic self-indulgence was made possible by the 'unearned' income on which he lived. As I have chosen to see him in this chapter, his vital, outgoing nature helps us to understand his love of arresting pictorial effects. The man's intuitive, physical exuberance and expansiveness are part of the warm, lyrical enjoyment that feeds the sonnets, however controlled their composition. François Coppée's description[33] of Heredia's sensual savouring of a book, statue, picture, ivory or bronze, matches Lavagne's account of Heredia's 'besoin de matérialisation orale'[34] when, at night, like Flaubert in his *gueuloir*, he read aloud, tasted in his mouth, judged with his ears and thereby sought to improve the subtle harmonies of his poems.[35] He did indeed have 'l'âme d'un enfant' if we mean that he sought to raise the child's capacity for absorption and its immediacy of enjoyment to the highest aesthetic level, to the consummate pleasure afforded by his sonnets. His child's soul refined by mature, intelligent discrimination gave primacy to the intense immediacy of the verbally beautiful as he, individually and privately, had experienced it.

II

THE POETRY

THE EARLY STAGES

All poets need some time to find what will eventually be seen as their authentic voice and preoccupations. Heredia did not take long: his contribution to the first *Parnasse contemporain* in 1866 was six sonnets ('Fleurs de feu', 'La Conque', 'Artémis', 'Les Scaliger', 'Prométhée', 'La Chasse') but well before then he was composing poems in that form, though he was not to consider them good enough to appear in *Les Trophées* in 1893. Heredia and the sonnet were therefore soon conjoined. But for a few years in the early 1860s, while trying his hand at some sonnets (only two of which, 'Pan' (1863) and 'La Mort de l'aigle' (1864), suitably modified, were included in *Les Trophées*), he revealed other influences, mainly Leconte de Lisle, Musset, Lamartine and Hugo but also his homonymic Cuban cousin, in compositions that by theme and form are far indeed from the dramatic succinctness usually associated with his name. Nature and love are their principal concerns. Our sources here are two-fold: those poems either unpublished or unacknowledged by Heredia and not taken up in *Les Trophées* but disclosed by others after his death and those quite unpublished manuscript poems to be found in the papers now in the Bibliothèque Nationale, the Bibliothèque de l'Arsenal and the Bibliothèque de l'Institut.[1] The *Poésies complètes* of 1924 (see Bibliography) contain some of these early poems, including those revealed by Ibrovac in his thesis, but the unpublished manuscripts not only yield others but also disclose misapprehensions by Ibrovac, e.g. the early poem 'A mon père dont les cheveux avaient blanchi avant l'âge', attributed to Heredia, is in fact a translation of a poem by his cousin.[2] The latter's influence—through certain themes like pride in Cuba and the Americas, Nature, the appeal of heroism and will-power—seems to be also present in an original early composition by the French José-Maria de Heredia, 'Les Bois américains', modestly sent from Cuba in 1860 to Fauvelle for his comments:[3] it is a set piece of fifty-six alexandrines which exotically depict the Cuban forests and sunset with the influence of Leconte de Lisle also evident at many points in both the vocabulary and the nirvana-like state evoked:

> L'esprit anéanti dans la Tranquillité
> Qui berce sur son sein rêveur la terre entière!

Six other poems—'C'était un soir d'été . . .', 'A une morte', 'Nuit d'été', 'Mars', 'Ballade sentimentale' and 'Chanson', composed between 1860 and 1862—evoke the young poet's powerful love for a mysterious Mlle de W . . .[4] whom he left in France in 1859 and who married while he was away in Cuba. We witness the Romantic gamut from initial intense infatuation to dejected, disabused abandonment in images and language that recall Lamartine and Musset:

> Nous nous tûmes longtemps.—La nuit et le silence
> Murmuraient à nos cœurs leur langage divin;
> Sa main, sans y songer, alla presser ma main;
> O premières amours! O souvenirs d'enfance!
>
> Alors en se levant avec un doux sourire,
> Comme ta Georgina dans le Saule, ô Musset,
> Elle dit d'une voix d'un pénétrant effet,
> Comme les flots plaintifs ou le vent qui soupire:
>
> 'Pâle étoile du soir, messagère lointaine . . .'
> —Et la nuit frissonnant dans les bois rafraîchis
> Versait ses flots d'argent sur les gazons blanchis,
> Et mon âme buvait sa volupté sereine.
>
> Quand elle soupirait: 'Un seul instant, arrête,
> Etoile de l'Amour, ne descends pas des cieux,'
> Sa voix tremblait, des pleurs avaient mouillé ses yeux,
> Sur mon sein frémissant elle pencha sa tête.
>
> Oh! qui me la rendra, l'illusion perdue?
> La jeunesse, la foi, l'espérance qui fuit?
> La céleste lueur a glissé dans la nuit,
> L'étoile de l'Amour du ciel est descendue.
>
> [. . .] Et moi qui t'aimais comme on adore Marie
> Quand on est tout enfant, d'un amour si pieux;
> Moi qui lisais ton cœur dans l'azur de tes yeux . . .
> Oh! je ne puis pleurer, car la source est tarie!
>
> (*P.C.*, pp. 225–7)

Heredia's young lady is a very close relation of Lamartine's time-stopping heroine in 'Le Lac' and the love expressed is as idealized and spiritualized as Lamartine's:

> Aimons-nous chastement, car c'est là qu'est la force [. . .]

> Il est beau de s'aimer d'un amour virginal,
> D'être deux dans le monde et ne faire qu'une âme,
> Et d'aller, confiant dans le cœur d'une femme,
> Appuyé sur l'amour conquérir l'idéal!
>
> (*P.C.*, p. 232)

Love is united with Nature's universal soul in a solar ecstasy that doubtless has something personal, of Cuba, in it and something of Lamartine and perhaps Hugo's pandemic raptures but in language that remains stiffly stereotyped:

> Tout fermente, tout vit; la nature inquiète
> Sent la sève et l'amour lui monter à la tête,
>   O frais et printanier réveil!
> O premières ardeurs! La terre, ivre, se noie
> Dans la blonde lumière et la féconde joie
>   Que verse à longs flots le soleil.
>
> (*P.C.*, p. 236)

Memories of Ronsard and the sixteenth-century expression of the classical theme of *carpe diem* (which Lamartine's 'Le Lac' had also exploited) are not far behind:

> La nature par là nous avertit, mignonne,
> De profiter du temps où notre âge fleuronne
>   En sa printanière saison;
> Car le cœur, dont aussi la virginité passe,
> Ne retrouve jamais la fraîcheur et la grâce
>   De sa première floraison.
>
> (*P.C.*, p. 236)

Even in these very early poems, where there is no hesitation in speaking in the first person and where the perspective is discreetly Musset-like ('jeune poitrine', 'taille mutine'), we already see Heredia distancing his feelings with repetition and refrain:

C'était un soir embaumé de printemps:
Tes yeux brillaient, et moi j'avais vingt ans!
Je te parlais, et sous la mousseline
Ton cœur battait dans ta jeune poitrine;
—Depuis ce jour qu'il s'est passé de temps!—
Et je pressais une taille mutine
Par un beau soir embaumé de printemps.

Tes yeux brillaient, et moi j'avais vingt ans!
Tout soupirait dans les prés éclatants [. . .]

(*P.C.*, p. 239)

These early poems are all strongly derivative, quite competent exercises by a very young poet opening up to life and love, searching for something to say and the way to say it. The influence of Musset in particular was marked in the early work of other young poets who were to become Parnassians, like Alphonse Daudet (*Les Amoureuses*, 1858) or Georges Lafenestre (*Les Espérances*, 1864). There is not the slightest indication here of the particular genius embodied in the later *Trophées*: it is precisely against this personal self-confession that Heredia will react, strongly and soon. But even among the limited number of early poems brought to light in 1923 by Ibrovac, there is a regular sonnet, dated 5 March 1860, Havana:

A la Fontaine de la India

Seul, quand finit le jour auprès de la fontaine,
J'aime à m'asseoir, rêvant à sa douce fraîcheur,
A laisser la pensée échapper de mon cœur,
Comme les gouttes d'eau de son urne trop pleine.

A la tiède splendeur de la lune sereine,
Sous ton blanc vêtement que traça le sculpteur,
Tu sembles t'animer, et ma charmante erreur
Prête des traits amis à ta forme incertaine.

O ma belle Indienne, amante du Soleil,
Que Colomb éveilla du virginal sommeil,
Où te berçait le chant des vagues amoureuses,

Cuba, ô mon pays, sous tes palmiers si beaux,
Qu'il est doux d'écouter la voix de tes ruisseaux,
Les murmures d'amour de tes nuits lumineuses!

(*P.C.*, p. 221)

If this is not a perfectly polished jewel it is a precious achievement for a seventeen-year-old: it has some of the lyrical power and control of the later sonnets, its partial humanization of the statue of the Indian girl adumbrates the later Parnassian manner and it shows Heredia finding the confidence to apostrophize his native island with love and a sense of pride in its historical perspective. It is a restrained anticipation of the eight sonnets to be published in 'Les Conquérants', a subsection of 'Le Moyen Âge et la Renaissance' in *Les Trophées* and doubtless owes something of its general inspiration to the patriotic poetry of Heredia's Cuban cousin. An early, undated and unpublished poem also composed in Cuba, 'Le Fils du Hatuey' ('Le Hatuey' being the name of a Cuban chieftain famous for his warlike exploits and patriotic ardour) also expresses a nascent pride in the young Heredia's birthplace:

> Amérique! Amérique! Aucun poëte encor
> N'a fait en ton honneur vibrer la harpe d'or;
> [. . .]
> Ecoute c'est un fils qui va chanter sa mère,
> Je suis un des enfants de tes vastes déserts;
> Aux accents les plus doux qu'ait entendus la terre,
> Je voudrais, mon pays, te bercer dans mes vers;[5]

Other early sonnets not to be taken up in *Les Trophées*— 'L'Héliotrope' (1862), 'Le Triomphe d'Iacchos' (1863) and the triptych of sonnets in 'Le Lis' (1863)—develop the theme of love already treated but, significantly, go a long way towards impersonalizing it. From the lily, symbol of virginity

> Il s'exhale, la nuit, de son large calice,
> Comme d'un encensoir, un parfum virginal!
> (*P.C.*, p. 247)

and despite the clichés and attitudinizing, the erotic climax already contains in germ the contrasts and intensity of feeling and expression to be found in many future sonnets:[6]

> Mais, un jour de désir, la vierge se pâmant
> Laissera profaner par la main de l'amant
> Tes fragiles trésors, Virginité sacrée!

Tel, au brûlant baiser de la brise égarée
Où flotte le pollen amoureux, s'enflammant
Le lis sème dans l'air sa poussière dorée!
(*P.C.*, p. 248)

The image of the intense solar heat that pours down on the helio-
trope is transformed into the poet's aspiration to be annihilated in
an erotic apotheosis or transfiguration:

Enfin, toute flétrie, elle demande l'ombre;
Mais le Dieu, la criblant de ses flèches sans nombre,
Lui verse sans pitié son implacable jour.

C'est après ce destin que soupire mon âme,
Et dût-elle en mourir, ah! verse-lui ta flamme,
Soleil ardent, soleil de l'invincible amour!
(*P.C.*, p. 245)

Both these sonnets, irregular in rhymes and later rejected, are well
on the way towards the themes and form of many sonnets in the
section 'La Grèce et la Sicile' in *Les Trophées*, while 'Le Triomphe
d'Iacchos', also irregular, explicitly embodies the young poet's
aspirations in the mythological figures of antiquity: some of the
words in this sonnet will go into the definitive 'Bacchanale' (1871)
of *Les Trophées* and the rest will be radically transformed to
become 'Ariane' (1863 and 1876). But one of the best of Heredia's
early sonnets to be published (unsigned, in the yearbook of *La
Conférence La Bruyère* 1861–2) is 'La Mort d'Agamemnon'. The
rhymes in its second quatrain were too irregular for it to merit
inclusion in *Les Trophées* but it is a remarkably early example of
Heredia's predilection for a dramatic picture with striking plastic
effects: it is his first *transposition d'art*, inspired by Pierre Guérin's
painting *Clytemnestre* in the Louvre:

Dans le fond du palais, sur sa couche d'airain,
Agamemnon repose et son âme se noie
Dans le divin sommeil; le souvenir de Troie
Vient à peine parfois plisser son front serein.

Il dort, et pour ses yeux le jour du lendemain
Ne luira pas. Le cœur plein de haine et de joie,
Clytemnestre déjà désigne de la main
A son timide amant cette royale proie.

Il tremble: ses cheveux se hérissent d'effroi;
Mais, vers le lit de pourpre où repose le roi,
L'enlaçant fortement d'une étreinte enivrante,

Elle le pousse; ils vont, sans haleine, à pas lents . . .
Egiste va frapper . . .Et la lampe mourante
Les éclaire tous deux de ses reflets sanglants.

(P.C., p. 244)

Certain traits here are quite worthy of the mature Heredia: the dramatic anticipation of ll. 5–6, the fierce antithesis, bordering on oxymoron, of 'cœur plein de haine et de joie' and of the picture in the finely concluded l. 8, the intense phsyiological detail in l. 9, the ecstatic near-climax at the end of l. 11, suspended at a key point in the sonnet to prepare for the full climax to crown the whole development with the murderous stab by Egisthus and the blood-red, pictorially resonant reflections in the last line. The qualities of this poem are surpassed at this early stage only by the sonnet 'Pan' which was published in the following year, 1863, in *La Revue française* almost in the final form it will have in *Les Trophées*.

The early date of 'Pan' and 'La Mort d'Agamemnon' shows the danger of any attempt to trace a gradual evolution of Heredia's talents and interests to the point where he can write sonnets which, with some modifications, will rank with his best. In these early years, he can suddenly reach very close to his later authentic manner and then move away to more tentative, derivative, though usually very interesting, exercises. The unpublished manuscripts confirm this impression. Early sonnets which have lain among his papers since he wrote them, probably dating from 1862, show the persistent influence of Leconte de Lisle as Heredia's imagination turns away for its inspiration from contemporary events towards the ideal of classical Greece. The references to sculpture in the second quatrain of the following poem are already Parnassian in their values:

Après avoir perdu votre grandeur, la terre
Vous resta douce, encor même sans liberté
Fils d'Hellas vous aviez l'amour de la beauté!
Dans l'azur sans limite, où vibrait la lumière

Vos rêves s'incarnaient dans l'ivoire ou la pierre-
L'Olympe descendait sur les fronts sculptés
Et vous pouviez du moins sans baisser la paupière
Voir palpiter vos Dieux dans les marbres domptés.

Aujourd'hui que pour nous Aphrodite est bien morte,
Et les autels déserts, que dans les cieux éteints
La splendeur ne luit plus des antiques matins,

L'Amour religieux du passé me transporte
Et dans la nuit immense où j'erre, le grand chœur
Des jours qui ne sont plus murmure dans mon cœur.[7]

Line 12—'L'Amour religieux du passé me transporte'—most explicitly and almost poignantly crystallizes the influence of Heredia's reading in the classics and his early studies in Paris as well as pointing the way to his future career as a poet who, with informed fervour, will seek to make the past come alive. Something of the same aspiration is expressed in the sonnet 'Vœu', published in November 1863 in *La Revue française*. To the initial quest for his own themes and his own manner, Heredia is beginning to find an answer. Yet another manuscript sonnet takes up the subject of singing the past with an even bolder commitment to celebrate in poetry its best and most glorious exploits, though the past envisaged this time is not ancient Greece but the medieval times of Charlemagne's knights:

Où donc est-il le temps des grandes équipées ?
Où donc les paladins? Dans quel cœur revivra
L'âme de ces héros que la gloire enivra
Lorsque retentissaient les vaillantes épées?

Durandal! Haute-Claire! au sang des rois trempée
Vous qui d'un large éclair que le luth célébra
Illuminez la nuit des sombres épopées,
Quel ouvrier nouveau jamais vous forgera?

O vieux siècles remplis d'héroïque aventure,
De crimes et d'amour, de gloire et forfaiture,
O vieux siècles de fer, admirables encor,

Je veux de vos hauts faits essayer la peinture,
Je veux vous faire vivre, et dans mes rimes d'or,
Te voir passer, Roland, colossale figure!

                    Paris 11 octobre 1862[8]

It is clear that heroic or epic perspective, rhetorical effect, dramatic intensity and the powerful *vers définitif* were an early acquired taste and practice for the young Heredia: their resonance doubtless echoed the yearnings of his passionate, ebullient temperament.

Yet other influences were still to have their effect on the evolving young poet. Among his papers, in a little green writing-book, on the inside cover of which Heredia inscribed 'Douarnenez 3 août 1864'—this seaside village in Brittany was already a favourite place for his holidays—there are two poems which owe nothing to the inspirations noted so far.[9] They suggest in their carefully wrought, arch simplicity as well as in the occasional element of refrain. a folk-lore quality which has not been glimpsed before:

> Ce fut au détour d'un sentier
> Que je rencontrai l'Inconnue,
> Un matin du printemps dernier.
> Depuis je ne l'ai pas revue.
>
> Autour de son front, ses cheveux
> S'éparpillaient en boucles folles;
> Frappé par l'éclair de ses yeux,
> Je restai tremblant, sans paroles.
>
> Elle avait si bien dans les bois
> Pillé les fleurs fraîches écloses,
> Qu'avec peine ses petits doigts
> Tenaient tant de bruyères roses.
>
> En me voyant tout interdit,
> L'enfant prit un brin de bruyère,
> Rougit un peu, me le tendit,
> Et se sauva, vive et légère.
>
> Je fus tout le jour en émoi;
> Depuis j'en ai l'âme inquiète.
> Je ne sais vraiment pourquoi
> Je garde encor cette fleurette?
>
> Douarnenez—20 août

Pourquoi?

Pourquoi détournez-vous les yeux,
Enfant, quand près de vous je passe?
Pourquoi vos regards gracieux
Eloignent-ils de moi leur grâce?
Pourquoi détournez-vous les yeux?

Pourquoi rougissez-vous sans cesse
Lorsque je vous parle tout bas?
Qu'ai-je pu dire qui vous blesse?
Pourquoi ne m'écoutez-vous pas?
Pourquoi rougissez-vous sans cesse?

Pourquoi me fuyez-vous ainsi
Sans que je puisse le comprendre?
Pourquoi me fuire, Mignonne, si
Je sais que vous veniez m'attendre?
Pourquoi me fuyez-vous ainsi?

Pourquoi pâlissez-vous sans cause,
Si parfois mon regard plus doux
Sur une autre que vous se pose?
Dites, pourquoi pâlissez-vous?
Pourquoi pâlissez-vous sans cause?
Paris 28 septembre 1864

Another poem, on a separate sheet, seems in comparable vein:

Chansonnette

Il est une chanson française,
Naïve et piquante à la fois,
Qui dit qu' à l'ombre des grands bois
Il fait bien bon cueillir la fraise,
Et se perdre aux sentiers ombreux,
    Quand on est deux.

Certes, si vous m'aimiez, Madame,
Sous ces grands bois que de bonheurs!
Qu'il est donc doux parmi les fleurs
Et les baisers perdre son âme,
Et de ce que disent les yeux
    Rougir tous deux!

Tenez! Regardez cette fraise;
Votre bouche est plus fraîche encor;
Vous rougissez, mon cher trésor;
Voulez-vous point que je la baise?
A quoi bon être scrupuleux
    Quand on est deux?

Ces marguerites effeuillées
Vous ont appris mon doux dessein:
Car je vois bondir votre sein,
J'entends sous les vertes feuillées
L'oiseau siffler: 'Il vaut bien mieux
    N'être que deux'!

Despite some clichés and clumsiness ('mon cher trésor'), these poems are moderately successful. Their inspiration is distinctive: partly a version of the classical and sixteenth-century *carpe diem*, retrospective nostalgia, fusion of artfulness and innocence particularly in questions asked to which the answers are transparent but unspoken, the woodland scene. It is too reminiscent of certain poems in Hugo's *Les Contemplations* (1856) for Heredia not to have been influenced by them.[10] It is useful to observe that he here showed interests and competence transcending the sonnet form and his later, characteristic themes, but he was not to develop this particular manner nor was he even to publish the three poems just quoted.

'LES CONQUERANTS DE L'OR' AND 'ROMANCERO'

Even *Les Trophées* of 1893 were not confined to the sonnet form. From the edition in the Athlone French Poets series we have excluded two epic compositions which were originally published in the same volume as *Les Trophées*; these can best receive attention now. 'LA DETRESSE D'ATAHUALLPA, Prologue: Les Conquérants de l'or' appeared in the second *Parnasse contemporain* of 1869. The New World and its conquest was to be a major source of inspiration for Heredia in both prose and poetry. His sonnet 'Les Conquérants' had already appeared in 1868 (*Sonnets et eaux-fortes*, Lemerre). For his 'Conquérants de l'or' Heredia used many details from W. H. Prescott's three-volume work on the conquest of Peru, but he was also familiar with other histories and accounts of the same subject[11]. His poem is a synthesis of his usual thorough knowledge and details from his imagination. 'Les Conquérants de l'or' was intended to be the prologue to a long epic poem about the conquest of Peru. The bastard Atahuallpa is briefly mentioned in section IV (l. 378) as having seized power over the Indians (in the north-west area of Peru) but 'Les Conquérants de l'or' is concerned only with the *conquistadores*. The poem ends as Pizarro is about to meet his victim Atahuallpa.

The first section serves mainly as an introduction, recounting briefly the expeditions that took place before 1522 in the Panama isthmus as far west and north as what is now Honduras and, to the east, as far as the river Orinoco, in what is now Venezuela. The whole section is a preparation for the entrance of the great Francisco Pizarro, whose expeditions to conquer Peru occupy the next five sections. From the start, he is pictured as the intrepid hero, of humble birth but noble soul, undaunted by the previous failures of others and by the fierce difficulties he encounters. Heredia depicts with obvious relish the horrors of Pizarro's first expedition (section II)—starvation, rain, reptiles and vampire bats. The second expedition takes him along the coast of what are now Colombia and Ecuador, which enables Heredia to dwell at some length on the tropical flora and fauna discovered: sandal-wood trees and forests of ebony and rosewood, the exotic birds and strange carnivores, the swarms of chattering monkeys in all their overwhelming variety. Pizarro reaches the northern end of the Andes and the gulf of Guayaquil and then the peace and riches of the Indian town of Tumbez. In section III, after his return to Panama because of depleted resources, Pizarro goes to Spain for authority and help: this interlude provides a dramatic confrontation between the doughty explorer and the Spanish emperor dazzled by the riches recounted by Pizarro. In section IV, Pizarro sallies forth again from Panama; Heredia uses the occasion to construct a colourful scene of prayers, adieux and pompous display. Pizarro reaches Tumbez again and begins the crossing of the Andes. The rest of section IV is a convincingly picturesque account of the awesome difficulties of these explorers' task. Section V is another exercise in exoticism : a rather too static roll-call of all the different members of the expedition. Section VI sees Pizarro and his men descend the eastern side of the Andes and the poem ends in the huzzas of the men saluting an appropriately grandiose sunset over the Andes.

'Les Conquérants de l'or' has some good descriptive passages but it is basically little more than a competent rhymed chronicle, a very different and inferior piece of poetry when set beside the sonnets in *Les Trophées*. In conception, it was doubtless an ambitious epic but remained quite unfinished; Heredia wryly called it his 'Panama' (Ibrovac, i, p. 275). The scale of things is very different from that of the sonnets. Using the traditional alexandrine with *rimes plates*, Heredia has the length and space for sustained and detailed epic narrative, he can develop large-scale effects at his ease. In consequence, though its subject and many of its passages are as heroically imposing as many of the sonnets, 'Les Conquérants de l'or', being less compact, is obviously slower in tempo than the sonnets and much less vividly dramatic.

Heredia's 'Romancero' is a unit of three poems: 'Le Serrement de mains' (49 lines), 'La Revanche de Diego Laynez' (49 lines) and 'Le Triomphe du Cid' (103 lines). It appeared in the *Revue des deux mondes* in 1885 but was begun as early as 1871. Enough has been seen of Heredia's interest and knowledge in respect of things Spanish—extending, of course, to South America—for these three episodes concerning El Cid to cause no surprise as themes. Yet in their form, the *terza rima*, and in their language, they mark a considerable break from the sonnets. *Romances* is the name given in Spanish to ballads; collections of them are called *romanceros*, of which there have been many. Various characters from Spanish history and legend figure in these *romances* and none more than the hero Ruy Díaz (Rodrigo, son of Diego), given the title Cid by the Moors (*Sayyid* meaning 'Master' in Arabic). He was born in Bivar, near Burgos, in or about the year 1040. His exploits as he fought against or with the Moors in Spain and acquired wealth and influence have extended into literature well beyond the *romances*. He presents many different faces, from gallant gentleman to barbarous brigand. Heredia's triptych is based on a limited part of this hero's early life, very familiar, however differently presented, through Corneille's *Le Cid*. The Cid's father, Diego Lainez, an old man, has received an insult from Count Gomez de Gormaz. The young man takes up his father's quarrel and kills the Count. The Count's daughter, Chimène, though she loves the Cid, asks the king for vengeance. According to Ibrovac, Heredia's source was the French translation by Damas Hinard, *Romancero espagnol ou recueil des chants populaires de l'Espagne* (two volumes, A. Delahaye, 1844). One source it undoubtedly was but Heredia could have availed himself of other editions and, of course, knowing Spanish so well, of the original *romances*.[12] Broadly speaking, he follows the original Spanish most closely in 'Le Serrement de mains', less closely in 'La Revanche de Diego Laynez' and most freely in 'Le Triomphe du Cid', the last episode being based on several *romances* and incorporating various changes and additions by Heredia. His choice of themes bears out one tendency we may note throughout *Les Trophées*, to seek what is violent, forceful, barbaric and exotic.

It is these traits which help to create the essentially dramatic or even melodramatic presentation in the first two episodes: the sombre old man, 'l'homme roidissant ses vieux muscles glacés', looking for one of his sons to avenge him, his histrionic and fierce handshake for each of the three elder sons, their contrasting replies full of feeble consternation, his contemptuous failure to reply. Climactic contrast is provided by the last and youngest son, the Cid, whose thin arms and white wrists are pointedly described as they are grasped by the father's, 'durcis par la guerre et le hâle'. The youngest and apparently most delicate son proves of course to be the bravest and toughest. Appropriately, his reply to his father as his young flesh feels the vice-like grip is more barbarously fierce than his brothers'. The laconic vigour of the father's orders is matched by the speedy action of the Cid and the dramatic brevity of the last line: 'Une heure après, Ruy Díaz avait tué le Comte'. 'La Revanche de Diego Laynez' goes even further in the same direction: the waiting, weeping father, the assumption that the Cid has been killed in his duel, the old man's imagined dishonour, the sudden return of the victorious son, and markedly enough, the victor's callous description of the loathsome object he has brought home, even more markedly, the actions of his father, rubbing his cheek with the clotted blood and slapping the corpseless head of the Count. The episode is closed on a nice *pointe* ('Car qui porte un tel chef est Chef de ma maison') taken straight from the original Spanish:

'Que quien trae cabeza/será en mi casa cabeza'. For the third episode, Heredia changes the place of assembly in the original *romance* from the palace at Burgos to Zamora, so that Chimène's complaint at her father's death can coincide with Rodrigue's triumphant return from victorious battles and hence the picturesque description of the acclaiming crowd. From his simple material, Heredia thus constructs a poem that again highlights the theatrically striking: heroic exploits, pathetic but vigorous intervention of Chimène, contrasting glances of the lovers, hesitations of the king Don Fernan, the—for Rodrigue—potentially dire choice Chimène is artfully offered, death of Rodrigue or acceptance of him. The ending is happy and tender, in best melodramatic style.

There is in this 'Romancero' much more local colour, e.g. place names, Rodrigue's famous sword 'Tizana', 'hidalgos', 'clercs', 'vilains', the booty brought back by Rodrigue, than quaintly archaic language, e.g. 'quérir', 'occire', 'chef' (cf. Ibrovac, ii, p. 416) but enough of both to enable Heredia to set his scenes and to concentrate on what for him are the essentials: passionate feeling, the muscularly energetic, significant stances and gestures. His three poems form an interesting comparison with Leconte de Lisle's 'La Ximena' and 'La Tête du Comte' (and also 'L'Accident de Don Iñigo'[13]); the two versions are often very close but, as Professor Fairlie observes, Heredia proves perhaps a better poet here than his master because there is less attempt by Heredia at archaism of style and less display of erudition. Colour, sound and dramatic effect are more in evidence in Heredia's poems and 'every physical impression is forced home to the uttermost'.[14] This is true of the slightest details: in 'Le Triomphe du Cid', Rodrigue's horse is 'rapide et rayé comme un zèbre', Chimène is 'sanglotante et pâmée,' his 'œil sombre' is set against her 'yeux clairs'. It is entirely characteristic that Heredia's controlled artistry should lead him to keep to the especially fixed form of the *terza rima* in all three episodes, whereas Leconte de Lisle uses it for only one of his, 'La Tête du Comte'. However stereotyped Heredia's 'Romancero' may seem now, it constitutes a very competent achievement, different from the rest of *Les Trophées* if below the level of his best sonnets. Both 'Les Conquérants de l'or' and 'Romancero' present another

embodiment of the aspiration we have noted in Heredia from
the early 1860s to celebrate the heroic and spectacular.

HEREDIA'S SONNETS: BACKGROUND AND INFLUENCES

When 'Les Conquérants de l'or' was published and the 'Romancero' begun, Heredia had no firmly established conception of the
contribution he was to make to the sonnet. But we have seen that
not only by his early compositions but by every natural tendency
and by every influence at work on him in his early years he was
strongly oriented towards the past. His training at the *Ecole des
Chartes* was one of the most important of these influences and it
gave him precise knowledge. The evolving Parnassian movement
was to be another, and the poetry that had nourished and pre-
pared it. French poetry in the nineteenth century and even, quite
simply, French literature at that time was often turned towards
the past. Chateaubriand was the great progenitor of the tendency
with his *Génie du christianisme* (1802) and the resurrection of the
Middle Ages. In poetry, Vigny (*Poèmes antiques et modernes*, 1826)
and Lamartine (*La Chute d'un ange*, 1830) in their very different
ways gave impetus to the epic viewpoint. The example of many
Parnassians, Leconte de Lisle (*Poèmes antiques*, 1852, *Poèmes
barbares*, 1862), the erudite Louis Ménard (*Poèmes*, 1855 and
Rêveries d'un païen mystique, 1876), Louis Bouilhet (*Mélænis*, 1851,
and *Festons et astragales*, 1859), Hugo (*La Légende des siècles*, 1859),
Théodore de Banville (*Les Cariatides*, 1842, *Les Stalactites*, 1846,
Les Exilés, 1868) reinforced Heredia's intuitive turning to earlier
ages, predominantly to Greece and Rome, but also to less distant
and more piquantly strange cultures. Others poets, like Léon
Dierx (*Poèmes*, 1864, *Les Lèvres closes*, 1867, and *Poésies complètes*,
1872) were to help to inspire particular themes like that of
Egypt, strengthening the impact of greater poets like Gautier.

A detailed study of the influences detectable in all Heredia's
sonnets would be quite beyond the scope of this study. A valiant
attempt was made in 1923 by Ibrovac, who devoted a whole
volume to *Les Sources des 'Trophées'*. The influences were many and
varied. For 'La Grèce et la Sicile', Heredia relied on his reading
of the classics, Virgil particularly, but the classics seen through
the poems of André Chénier, Hugo, Leconte de Lisle and Banville. The epigrams of the Greek Anthology were of particular

importance for this section (see our edition of *Les Trophées*, pp. 10–12). Certain contemporary prose writers fed Heredia with details and ideas: Paul Decharme (*Mythologie de la Grèce antique*, 1879), Paul de Saint-Victor (*Les Deux Masques*, 1880–4), Gaston Deschamps (*La Grèce d'aujourd'hui*, 1892). In 'Rome et les Barbares', Heredia's own wide reading again furnished the biggest contribution, his knowledge of Horace, Virgil, Catullus, Ovid, Juvenal, Martial and Livy but also his interest in archaeology and his noting of the inscription on a cippus discovered in Luchon (for 'Le Vœu') or a votive altar (for 'La Source'). In this section too, ancient times are seen through the work of major poets like Leconte de Lisle, Banville or Hugo. In 'Le Moyen Age et la Renaissance', the subsection 'Les Conquérants' seems an almost inevitable poetic flowering of Heredia's deep involvement in the history of Latin America so richly exemplified by his translation of Bernal Díaz (see below, Chapter III). For his evocation of the Middle Ages, certain key books were seminal: *Le Meuble en France au XVIe siècle*, 1887, by Edmond Bonnaffé—it also inspired 'Le Lit' in the section 'La Nature et le rêve'—*Recherches sur l'orfèvrerie en Espagne*, 1879, by Charles Davillier and *Un Condottiere au XVe siècle: Rimini*, 1882, by Charles Yriarte. Again, for this section as for 'L'Orient et les tropiques', the past is often seen through Heredia's reading of poets like Leconte de Lisle and Gautier, to the point that for the perceptive reader sufficiently acquainted with French poetry a given poem may seem to yield a veritable patchwork of influences, of ideas and even more of vocabulary; but in such cases each poem will usually embody several influences. As I have noted in our edition of *Les Trophées*, these debts are not so much borrowings as absorptions. Rhyme above all can become a crucial consideration: Ibrovac discloses a most acute memory and sensitivity as, linking rhyme and vocabulary, he sees reminiscences of past poets in many of the sonnets of *Les Trophées*. And for a poet whose talent lies so often in plastic effects, pictorial sources have considerable importance. The sonnet 'Le Tepidarium' in 'Rome et les Barbares' is closely modelled on Chassériau's painting similarly entitled, the sonnet 'Le Prisonnier' in 'L'Orient et les tropiques' is a verbal recreation of Gérôme's painting of the same name, while the Japanese influence in 'L'Orient et les tropiques' owes much, especially in

'Le Samouraï', to the illustrations and descriptions in Louis Gonse's two volumes, in 1883, on *L'Art japonais*. The painter Gustave Moreau certainly gave the inspiration for 'Némée', 'Stymphale' and 'Jason et Médée' while the Venetian landscape of 'La Dogaresse' condensed Heredia's impressions of Titian and Veronese.

Perhaps by 1866, certainly by 1872, Heredia had the notion that he would publish a collection of sonnets. But he did not spend twenty years seeking to clothe an initially established framework. It is true that the eventual structure of *Les Trophées* was partly implicit in the twenty-five 'sonnets héroïques' he published in the third *Parnasse contemporain* in 1876. The fact remains that he followed his interest or inspiration where it led him and that the unity of his preoccupations at a given moment is the sonnet he is seeking to perfect rather than a collection and certainly rather than anything he wanted to 'say'. As is shown in our edition, Heredia's concern was to give striking and memorable expression to events or things in the past which excited or moved him. This markedly impersonal poet was eminently personal in his basic inspiration and taste. The events may entail evocation of mythology ('La Grèce et la Sicile') or history ('Les Conquérants' or crucial battles and heroic figures in Roman times in 'Rome et les Barbares'), the things may be precious relics of the past, sword, stained-glass window, medallion or painting. Whether his fundamental inspiration is a person, event, scene or an *objet d'art*, his aim was always to create a sonnet, an *objet d'art* that was uniquely verbal. Some of his best sonnets, those that show his genius at its peak of maturity—like 'Nessus', 'La Centauresse', 'Centaures et Lapithes', 'La Trebbia' or the triptych on Anthony and Cleopatra—were not published until well into the 1880s. Since there is not space in this study to examine in detail the chronological development of Heredia's talent, we shall rather look at *Les Trophées* as a whole to determine the collection's principal qualities.

The history of the sonnet is long and honourable.[15] It seems to have originated in Sicily, at the court of whose king Frederick II the troubadours or Provençal poets gave the form its name and consecrated its usage in the course of the thirteenth century. From the beginning the sonnet was concerned with love and its anguishes; in the Italy of the thirteenth and fourteenth centuries, it was given a grave, intellectual quality by Dante and Petrarch. The first writers of sonnets in France were Marot and Saint-Gelais, in the third decade of the sixteenth century. By the middle of the century its use had spread. In these times the sonnet was in decasyllables. In the quatrains, *rimes embrassées* had triumphed over *rimes croisées* in fourteenth-century Italy. For the tercets, Marot favoured the rhyme-scheme CCDEED, with the consequence that this order of rhymes, as well as being called the Lyonnais arrangement, is also known as the *type de Marot*. The arrangement CCDEDE was first used in 1547 by Pelletier du Mans; of 117 sonnets in *Les Trophées*, 72 follow the latter rhyme-scheme in the tercets, while 31 have the Lyonnais arrangement. Pelletier du Mans was the guide and inspirer of the young Du Bellay who, with the sonnets of his collection *L'Olive* (1549) and, later, *Les Antiquités de Rome* (1558) and *Les Regrets* (1558) did much to give the form dignity, elegance, compactness, imaginative strength and wider themes such as moral and political concerns. Du Bellay's importance was matched by Ronsard's *Les Amours de Cassandre* (1552), *Les Amours de Marie* (1555), *Sonnets pour Hélène* (1578). Through the famous *Pléiade*, they were to promote the recommendations of Du Bellay's *Défense et illustration de la langue française* (1549), some of which Heredia, who had a deep love for both these Renaissance poets,[16] was to espouse three hundred years later: the imitation of classical literary models (Du Bellay was more the Latinist, Ronsard the Hellenist, but both poets, like Heredia, turned to both classical cultures), a prefiguration of the Parnassian attachment to the *mot juste* in the adoption of terms used by craftmen, the importance of effort and deliberate art. In Ronsard's sonnets especially, Heredia found the wealth of classical and mythological allusion which was to characterize many of his own poems. Two other important modifications to the sonnet were assured by Du Bellay and Ronsard: the admission of the alexandrine instead of the decasyllable and the *alternance des rimes*. By 1560, both changes had received widespread adoption.

After its flowering in the hands of Ronsard and Du Bellay, the sonnet became one of the most popular verse-forms and its subject-matter was widened to include almost anything, from the most serious to the most, and sometimes wittily, futile. The esteem in which it came to be held is illustrated by the famous quarrel in 1649 between the Jobelins and Uraniens. The poet Benserade, attached to the house of Condé, had accompanied a paraphrase of the book of Job, sent to a lady, with a sonnet which was much praised. Not to be outdone, the house of Longueville produced a sonnet by Voiture, who was its accredited poet, addressed to a lady named Uranie. The relative merits of the two sonnets became a burning issue at court and in polite society, dividing those involved into two sets of protagonists, Jobelins and Uraniens. Such fame for a couple of sonnets was perhaps a more novel tribute than the instances recorded of financial reward—3000 *livres* given by Richelieu to Achillini for his sonnet on the capture of La Rochelle or the 30,000 *livres* bestowed by Henri IV on Desportes for his sonnet on Diana and Hippolytus.

The sonnet seemed doomed to go into a decline by its excessive virtuosity and ingenuity. After 1660, it became less common. Boileau praised it but stressed its difficulty: few then wrote in the form. Its next great renaissance was to be in the nineteenth century. It was Sainte-Beuve, the exhumer of Du Bellay and Ronsard in his *Tableau historique et critique de la poésie française au XVIe siècle* (1828), who began the return to popularity in his *Poésies de Joseph Delorme* (1829) and *Les Consolations* (1830). No great poet by either natural talent or careful effort, Sainte-Beuve nevertheless found his own small inspiration in themes of inadequacy and dissatisfaction with psychologically well-founded detail. Amid the relative neglect of the form among Romantic poets, Auguste Barbier is an exception who was to be remembered later in the century, the first to attempt a cycle of epic sonnets. He was the author of *Il Pianto* (1833), which contains eleven sonnets with themes like Michelangelo, Raphael, Corregio, Cimarosa, Titian and Leonardo da Vinci and, more importantly, of *Rimes héroïques* (1843), thirty-one sonnets on a succession of great historical figures from Sainte-Geneviève to Christ. Barbier was to publish in the second *Parnasse contemporain* of 1869. Though not to be affected by this poet's early social preoccupations, Heredia noted not just the ringing adjective of the title *Rimes héroïques*, which would evoke such a personal response from him (cf. Heredia's own 'sonnets héroïques' in the third *Parnasse contemporain*), but Barbier's original combination of epic themes with the particular form of the sonnet. The combination received specific comment in the preface to *Rimes héroïques* in a manner calculated to challenge the young Heredia of twenty years later:

> Ce petit poëme d'invention moderne a le mérite d'encadrer avec précision l'idée ou le sentiment. Il se prête à tous les tons; et, quoique accoutumé à soupirer les peines du cœur et à exhaler les tristesses de l'âme, il peut monter aux notes les plus fières, et faire entendre les accents les plus mâles.

The example and influence of Banville's *Les Cariatides* (1842) and *Les Stalactites* (1846) have already been noted. Though the first collection contained only six sonnets and the second just one, all seven sonnets were very good by later Parnassian standards, sumptuous in theme and style with sonorous rhymes. Banville was to be a very strong upholder of discipline and regularity in the sonnet, as he revealed in his *Petit Traité de versification française* (1872). 1857 seems to have been a crucial year. It saw the publication of Banville's *Le Sang de la coupe* with nine sonnets, seven of which with their evocation of heroic Grecian figures like the Amazons or Jason and the Argonauts undoubtedly made a great impression on Heredia. In the same year, the first edition of Baudelaire's *Les Fleurs du mal* offered forty-four sonnets out of a total of a hundred and one poems. Baudelaire's use of the sonnet was much more free and flexible than Heredia's and his subject-matter was not to influence Heredia in any marked way, but the sonnet's return to the centre of poets' attention could be said to be assured. The emergence of the Parnassian poets and the three editions of the *Parnasse contemporain* consecrated this return in which Heredia was to play such an important part. The first *Parnasse contemporain* of 1866 contained eighty sonnets, six of them by Heredia; his contribution to the third *Parnasse contemporain*, we have already seen, will be twenty-five. In 1868 appeared Lemerre's *Sonnets et eaux-fortes*, containing etchings from contemporary artists such as Corot, Gérôme, Millet and Manet. Each etching was set opposite a sonnet by one of the poets who had collaborated in the first *Parnasse contemporain* or who was due to contribute to the second in 1869. The magnificent luxury of this publication, with its association of the sonnet and pictorial art, embodied the triumph of both *Le Parnasse* and of the sonnet, unless we regard the sonnet as reaching an even greater point of glory in 1890 when the review *La Plume* organized a sonnet competition and received 145 from every part of France. 1874 saw the appearance of the *Livre des sonnets* (Lemerre), with its 100 sonnets (republished in 1875 with 140 sonnets), prefaced by the *Histoire du sonnet* by Charles Asselineau which had first appeared in 1856 and had helped to strengthen Heredia's ambition to write in this form. By now, almost all poets seemed to be composing sonnets.

LES TROPHEES

In poetry, as in much else, perspective is all-important. For some readers of *Les Trophées*—more commonly, one is glad to reflect, those at the turn of the century than those in more recent times— a main danger has been to see the collection too much as a kind of decoratively versified history course. In this perspective, *Les Trophées* is an impressive pageant evoking a whole sweep of time from the ancient civilizations of Egypt through ancient Greece and Rome to the sixteenth century of Spain, Latin America, the Renaissance of Italy and France in all its heroic finery and sometimes murderous savagery, with some more personal evocations of contemporary life in 'La Nature et le rêve'. By this view, Heredia brings out the heroic quality of Man throughout the ages, his efforts to transcend normal human limitations, embodied in mythological figures like Hercules, in historical leaders like Hannibal, Mark Anthony and the *conquistadores* or in outstanding artists such as Ronsard, Benvenuto Cellini, Michelangelo or Claudius Popelin. Hence some of the most exuberantly energetic sonnets in the French language, like 'Némée' or 'Soir de bataille'. For this exultant panorama of Man the backcloth is Nature, land or sea, often forgotten or neglected by Man yet fundamentally soothing in its apparently eternal witness, with the consequent impression of the permanence and regularity of certain laws cyclically relived by succeeding generations. 'Tout meurt' ('Sur le Livre des Amours de Pierre de Ronsard' in 'Le Moyen Age et la Renaissance'), 'Le temps passe. Tout meurt. Le marbre même s'use' ('Médaille antique' in 'La

Nature et le rêve'): men, civilizations, even gods pass away. Such eternal verities have been reiterated by thinkers and poets for thousands of years: in *Les Trophées* they provide for the exuberant heroism just evoked a concluding melancholy and even pessimism which is nevertheless sober, calm and controlled. Few resurrections of the past, entailing our apparent defeat by time, can avoid a measure of sadness, but Heredia's sadness is given a noble serenity by the consolation derived from the very expressive beauty of art. Explicitly and, above all, implicitly, by the achievement of his art, Heredia is linked in a family which from Horace, Virgil or the authors of the Greek Anthology extends to the Pléiade, Gautier, Baudelaire, Mallarmé and other great poets.

This perspective is not so much wrong as incomplete. The subject-matter of Heredia's sonnets is indeed as indicated. It is the field of ideas and impressions in which he composes. But, as we noted in our first chapter, *fond* in poetry is inseparable from *forme* so that it would be more accurate to say that we have just described a field of ideas *from* which, rather than *in* which, Heredia composes. The historical or ideological perspective does not take sufficient account of the compactness and concentration that have ensured the sonnet's attraction for hundreds of years. Fourteen lines of alexandrines with a very limited choice of rhyme-schemes allows no room for indecisiveness in the poet nor for padding, which is always cruelly exposed by so compressed a medium. Careful artistry and management of effects are implicit in the very nature of the sonnet. From his first attempts, Heredia's strength and originality lay in the marriage of the ostensibly opposed: a short, limited, tightly structured verse-form and themes that are epic, with potentially immense resonances and therefore, so to speak, straining to break out of the sonnet form. This inherent tension of Heredia's sonnet complements the contrasting tension set up in himself, between the ebullient expansiveness of his temperament and the constricting, impersonal precision of the form in which he chose to write.

Tension and contrast are the stuff of drama. What the historical perspective given earlier most undervalues is what in the introduction to our edition of *Les Trophées* I have called 'dramatic immediacy' or 'dramatic dynamism'. Such phrases are attempts to capture the essential, lyrical virtue of Heredia's sonnets, which is to convey as immediately as possible a range of effects which, for purposes of analysis and understanding, have to be considered separately.

Speech is one integral part of the dramatic dynamism in *Les Trophées*. It takes different forms: direct address from a given character, usually from the subject of the poem, as in 'Hortorum Deus' ('Rome et les Barbares'), and, where possible, from a piquantly paradoxical source, as in 'La Prière du mort' ('La Grèce et la Sicile'), where it is the dead man who addresses the passer-by and therefore us or direct address from the poet, either to us or to Nature, and occasionally conversation between characters. Apostrophe is the commonest device employed to give the immediacy of direct speech; its role is vital when the theme risked being static, as in 'L'Epée' and 'Email' ('Le Moyen Age et la Renaissance'). But the ramifications of the dramatic extend much further. Normally slow processes are speeded up or given greater urgency by the power communicated to them, like the flowering aloe in 'Fleur séculaire' ('L'Orient et les tropiques'). Words conveying action and movement and especially, of course, verbs are carefully used to make the inanimate as active as possible. Even more importantly, it is as miniature dramas that the sonnets excel, especially the *sonnets antiques* of 'La Grèce et la Sicile' such as all those involving Hercules and Perseus. The character or event being intrinsically dramatic, Heredia's art is to bring out this quality to the utmost. He does this by selecting a significant moment—Pan seizing a nymph, Perseus swooping down to rescue Andromeda, Ariadne about to be embraced by the triumphant Bacchus—usually devoting the quatrains, and sometimes the first tercet as well, to the depiction of significant background detail so that the later part of the sonnet can end on an exciting or resonant climax. Such miniature dramas often entail two further characteristics: the art of perspective, implying, as in 'La Trebbia' ('Rome et les Barbares'), the various levels of activity in foreground, middle ground and distance and, a much more favourite procedure, the art of holding back for effect not just the climax leading to the *vers définitif* but the name of the protagonist or the explanation of an impressive effect already described; inversion is frequently used to strengthen

this device of postponement by giving greater force to the words
coming later. It is sometimes suggested that the main function
of the first thirteen lines of an Heredia sonnet is to lead into the
climactic last line. I have suggested in the introduction to our
edition of *Les Trophées* that though there is a grain of truth in
such a suggestion, it takes no account of the variety of *vers
définitifs* in *Les Trophées*. (See Athlone French Poets edition, p. 27).
Antithesis of many kinds, working at different levels, is perhaps
the most frequent dramatic device used in *Les Trophées*, from the
evocation of a scene as it is now in contrast with what it once was,
seen at its best in a sonnet such as 'A une ville morte' ('Le
Moyen Age et la Renaissance'), to the contrast between noise and
silence in 'La Trebbia' ('Rome et les Barbares'). Greater force
can be given by describing the time before or after some important
event: 'La Trebbia' is set before the battle, 'Après Cannes' in the
same section comes after a battle, so that we have concentration
on expectancy and consternation. Interplay of light and shade, of
colours and shapes, is another facet of the power of contrast in
Heredia's collection, as is the fondness for oxymoron, the fusion
of opposites in an unusually arresting climax. 'Silencieusement
vers le soleil aboie' ('La Vision de Khèm I' in 'L'Orient et les
tropiques') is a verbal equivalent to the controlled, ecstatic
discord at the end of a powerful musical development as in the
last movement of Beethoven's *Leonora*, III overture. All these
aspects of Heredia's dramatic dynamism are best appreciated at
the level of the individual sonnet and in that context: it is hoped
that the commentaries in our edition of *Les Trophées* will be
particularly useful in this respect.

It seems at this point appropriate to compare sonnets by
Barbier, Banville and Heredia to see how Heredia differed from
his predecessors. I give first one of Barbier's poems from *Il
Pianto* (1833), followed by Heredia's on the same theme, first
published just before *Les Trophées* at the beginning of 1893:

Michel-Ange

Que ton visage est triste et ton front amaigri,
Sublime Michel-Ange, ô vieux tailleur de pierre!
Nulle larme jamais n'a mouillé ta paupière:
Comme Dante, on dirait que tu n'as jamais ri.

Hélas! d'un lait trop fort la Muse t'a nourri,
L'art fut ton seul amour et prit ta vie entière;
Soixante ans tu courus une triple carrière
Sans reposer ton cœur sur un cœur attendri.

Pauvre Buonarroti! ton seul bonheur au monde
Fut d'imprimer au marbre une grandeur profonde,
Et, puissant comme Dieu, d'effrayer comme lui:

Aussi, quand tu parvins à ta saison dernière,
Vieux lion fatigué, sous ta blanche crinière,
Tu mourus longuement plein de gloire et d'ennui.

Michel-Ange

Certe, il était hanté d'un tragique tourment,
Alors qu'à la Sixtine et loin de Rome en fêtes,
Solitaire, il peignait Sibylles et Prophètes
Et, sur le sombre mur, le dernier Jugement.

Il écoutait en lui pleurer obstinément,
Titan que son désir enchaîne aux plus hauts faîtes,
La Patrie et l'Amour, la Gloire et leurs défaites;
Il songeait que tout meurt et que le rêve ment.

Aussi ces lourds Géants, las de leur force exsangue,
Ces Esclaves qu'étreint une infrangible gangue,
Comme il les a tordus d'une étrange façon;

Et dans les marbres froids où bout son âme altière,
Comme il a fait courir avec un grand frisson
La colère d'un Dieu vaincu par la Matière!

With excellent unity of purpose and effect, Barbier's poem stresses the awesome devotion of the great artist to his solitary calling and ends on a resonant climax harmonizing 'gloire' and 'ennui' in a verbal chord that Baudelaire and Heredia would not have wanted to disavow. There is also an impressive combination of strength and ease in the sonnet's rhythms. Heredia's sonnet is not one of his best but its unity is as strong as Barbier's, with its concentration on Michelangelo's 'tragique tourment', the anguish caused by the artist's longing to achieve perfect expression which is finally defeated by the intractability of matter. Heredia's language can be more incisive (l. 8), his images in the sestet (particularly in the startling contrast in l. 12—'marbres *froids* où *bout*') are more restlessly urgent than Barbier's, his whole sonnet is further away from the quality of *récit* in Barbier, more intensely and dramatically compact.

The first of the next two sonnets is from Banville's *Les Princesses* (1874) and the other one of Heredia's evocations from 'Persée et Andromède' ('La Grèce et la Sicile'), first published in 1885:

Andromède

Andromède gémit dans le désert sans voile,
Nue et pâle, tordant ses bras sur le rocher.
Rien sur le sable ardent que la mer vient lécher,
Rien! pas même un chasseur dans un abri de toile.

Rien sur le sable, et sur la mer pas une voile!
Le soleil la déchire, impitoyable archer,
Et le monstre bondit comme pour s'approcher
De la vierge qui meurt, plus blanche qu'une étoile.

Ame enfantine et douce elle agonise, hélas!
Mais Persée aux beaux yeux, le meurtrier d'Atlas,
Vient et fend l'air, monté sur le divin Pégase.

Il vient, échevelé, tenant son glaive d'or,
Et la jeune princesse, immobile d'extase,
Suit des yeux dans l'azur son formidable essor.

Andromède au monstre

La Vierge Céphéenne, hélas! encor vivante,
Liée, échevelée, au roc des noirs îlots,
Se lamente en tordant de vains sanglots
Sa chair royale où court un frisson d'épouvante.

L'Océan monstrueux que la tempête évente
Crache à ses pieds glacés l'âcre bave des flots,
Et partout elle voit, à travers ses cils clos,
Bâiller la gueule glauque, innombrable et mouvante.

Tel qu'un éclat de foudre en un ciel sans éclair,
Tout à coup, retentit un hennissement clair.
Ses yeux s'ouvrent. L'horreur les emplit, et l'extase;

Car elle a vu, d'un vol vertigineux et sûr,
Se cabrant sous le poids du fils de Zeus, Pégase
Allonger sur la mer sa grande ombre d'azur.

Banville's sonnet is good, with a fine climax. It is perhaps rather unsure of itself with the repetitions in ll.3–5. The detail in l. 4 hardly seems well chosen. The movement from Andromeda to Perseus comes a little uneasily in l. 10 when the first line of the first tercet has already been taken up with a summary of Andromeda's abject position, but this placing, it can be argued, is for greater contrast before the climax. Heredia's sonnet owes much to Banville's in conception and even in vocabulary. The word 'extase' is particularly important, but the borrowed word 'échevelé' is surely better transferred from Perseus to Andromeda, for psychological reasons. As I hope is shown by the commentary on Heredia's poem in our edition, its detail is more tellingly compact, its structure and whole execution more dramatically ordered, its evocation of both Andromeda and Perseus more zestfully and energetically powerful.

In the same collection of *Les Princesses* Banville offered his 'Cléopâtre', another good poem full of cogent and plastically exotic, even barbarous, details. Again, however, the nearest equivalent in Heredia—'Le Cydnus' ('Rome et les Barbares'), first published in 1884—is denser, more dramatic, with its concentration on Cleopatra's rapacious dominance and the telling contrast between her and Mark Anthony weakened by love. No line in Banville's sonnet is as lyrically incantatory as Heredia's 'Ses bras d'ambre où la pourpre a mis des reflets roses':

Cléopâtre

Dans la nuit brûlante où la plainte continue
Du fleuve pleure, avec son grand peuple éternel
De dieux, le palais, rêve effroyable et réel,
Se dresse, et les sphinx noirs songent dans l'avenue.

La blanche lune, au haut de son vol parvenue,
Baignant les escaliers élancés en plein ciel,
Baise un lit rose où, dans l'éclat surnaturel
De sa divinité, dort CLEOPATRE nue.

Et tandis qu'elle dort, délices et bourreau
Du monde, un dieu de jaspe à tête de taureau
Se penche, et voit son sein où la clarté se pose.

Sur ce sein, tous les feux dans son sang recélés
Etincellent, montrant leur braise ardente et rose,
Et l'idole de jaspe en a les yeux brûlés.

Le Cydnus

Sous l'azur triomphal, au soleil qui flamboie,
La trirème d'argent blanchit le fleuve noir
Et son sillage y laisse un parfum d'encensoir
Avec des sons de flûte et des frissons de soie.

A la proue éclatante où l'épervier s'éploie,
Hors de son dais royal se penchant pour mieux voir,
Cléopâtre debout en la splendeur du soir
Semble un grand oiseau d'or qui guette au loin sa proie.

Voici Tarse, où l'attend le guerrier désarmé;
Et la brune Lagide ouvre dans l'air charmé
Ses bras d'ambre où la pourpre a mis des reflets roses;

Et ses yeux n'ont pas vu, présages de son sort,
Auprès d'elle, effeuillant sur l'eau sombre des roses,
Les deux Enfants divins, le Désir et la Mort.

We all run the risk of having our attention so taken by those sonnets in *Les Trophées*—like the subsection 'Hercule et les Centaures' or 'Persée et Andromède' in 'La Grèce et la Sicile', a limited number of poems in 'Rome et les Barbares', nearly all in 'L'Orient et les tropiques' and several in 'La Nature et le rêve'— which most vividly and, in terms of sound, most resonantly, embody the qualities to which we have referred that we tend to neglect the others which also illustrate what we have called dramatic immediacy but which are much more quietly beautiful, like those of the subsection 'Epigrammes et Bucoliques' in 'La Grèce et la Sicile' or the 'Sonnets épigraphiques' in 'Rome et les Barbares'. Their relative restraint is such that Heredia can legitimately be described as an elegiac poet, adept in fusing gentleness, calm, nostalgia and the sadness of things. It is when we bear in mind all his sonnets that we are led to see the vital role of Heredia's rich vocabulary, his deployment of *mots justes* from various contexts, some of the most important being bookbinding, diamond-work, jewellery and the work of the goldsmith, war and heraldry. His adjectives vary from the strikingly original (like 'calme granitique' and the later 'rêve granitique' in 'La Vision de Khèm II', in 'L'Orient et les tropiques') to the general and universal. Heinrich Fromm[17] pointed out that the adjectives most used in *Les Trophées* are *grand, vieux, sombre, beau;* the frequency of such unspecific adjectives, like that of tautology and periphrasis, is unsurprising in a poet so concerned to depict what he sees as the more or less unchanging nature of man and life (see p. 68).

The role of versification and the particular use made by Heredia of the alexandrine are best examined in specific instances from individual sonnets.[18] Sound effects are complex and difficult to assess, while the impressions they create can be notoriously subjective. If cases of *enjambement* and *rejet* are not very frequent in *Les Trophées*, they are important when they do occur, especially for emphasis. There is no *enjambement* between stanzas, that is, between quatrains and tercets. This may seem curiously inflexible by comparison with Baudelaire or Verlaine, but it is part of Heredia's traditional *tenue* and is linked with his power of firm, clear, striking evocation. His alexandrines are usually binary but, as in Racine, there is great variation in the placing of accents in the body of the line, usually with the most successful consequences. Alliteration and assonance are among his most marked characteristics, sometimes to an exceptionally intense degree (like 'Le troupeau monstrueux en renâclant recule' in 'Centaures et Lapithes' from the section 'La Grèce et la Sicile'): they embody the intrinsic pleasure to be found in such handling of words, quite apart from any imitative effect they are sometimes thought to have. As has been pointed out in our edition (p. 25), about half of his rhymes are 'rich', if by rich we mean words having in common the *consonne d'appui* and two other elements, voiced consonant or vowel. In fact, what many Parnassians looked for was not only richness of rhyme but also avoidance of banal, too obvious, rhymes; in this pursuit, Heredia is quite successful much of the time.

In the matter of the sonnet's versification, it is interesting to note that, for the quatrains, Heredia took a few years to follow with complete rigour the traditional pattern of repeated *rimes embrassées*: ABBA ABBA. Of the twenty-four sonnets he published between 1861 and 1868, only six were regular. He explained with some humour how Théophile Gautier reproached him in those early days with the composition of such *sonnets libertins* and how he resolved to write no more.[19] The quatrains in every sonnet in *Les Trophées* rhyme ABBA ABBA. The rhymes of the tercets show some limited variety: 72 have CCDEDE, the pattern favoured by Ronsard and Banville, 31 CCDEED, the old Lyonnais pattern, 7 have CDDCEE, 3 CDCDEE, 2 CDCDCD, 1 CDDCDC and 1 CCDDCD. All the patterns had been used before Heredia. He favoured CCDCCD in the early part of his career but CCDEDE increasingly became his chosen pattern as the years went by. For most of us, the more important facts to note are that Heredia seems to have concentrated his best efforts on the sestet: it was with this part of the sonnet that he usually began composition. Structurally speaking, the quatrains, or the quatrains with the first tercet, usually set the scene, often with images striking or effective enough, but it is in the sestet or the second tercet that we reach the sonnet's most crucial part: the climax, the explanation, the conclusion. The relating of quatrains and tercets is fairly stereotyped and detectable, as noted by Thauziès (see Bibliography): *Aujourd'hui . . ., C'est pourquoi . . ., Viens . . ., Partons . . ., Il a vu . . .* and also, as Ibrovac observes (ii, p. 491), *C'est alors . . ., C'est l'heure . . .* and, above all, *Car. . . .* If this range seems too limited, readers should try to write sonnets to appreciate the difficulties of the transition between the octet and sestet!

There is no verse-form less suited than the sonnet to those poets who have more vague yearnings than sensitive skill to express them. Heredia had the maturity to realize that, in Valéry's aphorism, 'les mauvais vers sont faits de bonnes intentions'. He had both the passion and the patience to bring the sonnet to a point of perfection within the context of his own preoccupations and temperament. In 1894, speaking for the Académie française at the inauguration of a statue to one of France's earliest and greatest sonneteers, he summed up the nature of the sonnet and Du Bellay's achievement in a few terse sentences that he thoroughly deserves to have applied to himself:

Le sonnet, par la solide élégance de sa structure et par sa beauté mystique et mathématique, est sans contredit le plus parfait des poèmes à forme fixe. Elliptique et concis, d'une composition logiquement déduite, il exige du poète, dans le choix du peu de mots où doit se concentrer l'idée et des rimes difficiles et précieuses, un goût très sûr, une singulière maîtrise. Or nul, ni même Ronsard n'a su faire tenir, dans le cadre étroit de ces quatorze vers, des tableaux d'un art si accompli, aussi puissant que délicat, où l'ingéniosité la plus raffinée s'unit à la plus mâle et à la plus exquise simplicité.[20]

III

OTHER WORKS

The occasional poems other than sonnets composed by Heredia (see *P.C.*) show that he could use other forms and sometimes with success. They disclose themes that remain eminently theatrical, often deriving from his Spanish ancestry. Whatever interest or merit such poems may offer, they seem to confirm Heredia's wisdom in concentrating his inspiration mostly in the sonnet form which helped to give it truly consummate expression. We reflect that, in poetry, he expressed himself with greater concentration by being the author of only one collection of poems. In prose, he produced no truly original work of importance. There were speeches, prefaces, some interviews and other occasional writings which are a considerable aid to our understanding of his taste and competence (see Bibliography). His edition of André Chénier's *Bucoliques* and his translations from the Spanish are especially revealing and merit particular examination: they reinforce a general impression given by all his writing, prose as well as verse, of reticence and careful erudition. It would have been alien to all his values not only to attach importance in his compositions to the events of his own life but even to promote in too directly personal terms the things and people he loved. It has already been suggested, in our first chapter, that he was too stable and his interests too directed away from self for him to feel any need for such self-promotion. Instead, a former student of the *Ecole des Chartes* acquits a personal debt of love and admiration by editing Leconte de Lisle and Chénier and by works of translation that enabled him to indulge and express in the most objective manner his open-hearted interest in the variety of the world as well as in the heroic and the exotic. And this generalization carries its dangers because his translation of *Juan Soldado* embodies a sense of the comic and the absurd likely to surprise many lovers of the sonnets.

EDITIONS AND OCCASIONAL WRITINGS

Heredia's edition, in collaboration with the vicomte de Guerne, of Leconte de Lisle's *Derniers poèmes* (Lemerre, 1895) carefully produces the text of the poems and all we read of Heredia himself is one prefatory sentence explaining that this edition was a devout duty:

> Leconte de Lisle ayant manifesté le désir que la publication de ses œuvres posthumes nous fût confiée, nous y avons apporté le soin pieux que devaient à sa chère et illustre mémoire notre reconnaissance et notre admiration.

His edition of André Chénier's *Les Bucoliques* (Maison du livre, 1905) is a more important publication because it reveals an influence on Heredia that is perhaps less apparent and less well known than that of the leader of the Parnassian poets and because 'Le Manuscrit des *Bucoliques*' offers a detailed account of how and why Heredia assumed his task. He clearly took great pains reading the manuscript again and again as well as what had been written on Chénier. He compares the work of deciphering the manuscript to that of someone bringing together the remains of some statue by Scopas or Polycletes. His approach is firmly methodical, yet wedded to all that he can assemble by way of intuitive sympathy:

> Pour faire des *Bucoliques* l'édition idéale rêvée par Sainte-Beuve, pour en faire *un livre*, la grande, la seule difficulté à vaincre, était de trouver ou, pour mieux dire, d'imaginer une classification logique et claire. A première vue, le problème paraît insoluble. Débrouiller le chaos, quelque admirable qu'il soit, semble impossible à qui n'est pas un dieu. Mais l'homme, s'il n'est pas éternel, peut être patient. L'amour et la patience unis sont bien forts. A force d'y songer, de lire, de relire les manuscrits, je parvins peu à peu à les classer, quoique bien vaguement encore, dans mon esprit.

'Le Manuscrit des *Bucoliques*' appeared in 1905, one month after Heredia died. The views he expresses were therefore the culmination of a life's reading and writing. The love and influence of Chénier had been so great that when Heredia went into the details of Chénier's versification he could almost be explaining his own practice. From an early age, Heredia nourished a particular regard for the forty-four lines in Chénier's poem 'L'Aveugle' which evoke the struggle between the Lapiths and the Centaurs: several sonnets in *Les Trophées* show evidence of this influence.[1] But the taste shared with Chénier is not just for a certain mythological theme. What attracts Heredia is the *coupes* of Chénier's alexandrines, the intensely dramatic effects of his stylised precipitateness:

> Le vers y va par bonds, heurts, chocs et soubresauts. Il s'arrête, il reprend brusquement. Et, par son allure haletante, saccadée, en une suite de traits où sont accumulés et variés les artifices du plus admirable métier, il fait percevoir du même coup à l'œil, à l'oreille et à l'esprit tout le désordre furieux de cette héroïque mêlée.
>
> Mais c'est surtout aux ellipses violentes, à ces latinismes hardis, aux souples inversions, aux dérèglements de syntaxe où son libre génie s'irrite et se joue, qu'André Chénier, conscient de ses audaces, les a voulu plus indélébilement marquer par sa ponctuation. Elle est grossie à dessein, comme burinée.

Dramatic strength and sharp, clear outlines thus appeal to both poets. Given this conformity of taste, it is understandable that Heredia draws attention to those aspects of Chénier's poetic genius which, even more cogently, he exemplifies himself, in particular, the capacity for dramatic, objective, pictorial evocation in which landscapes and figures reinforce each other. The following description of Chénier would just as well apply to Heredia himself:

> Son génie est essentiellement objectif et dramatique. Il a, à la plus haute puissance, le don d'évocation, la première des vertus poétiques. Il se dédouble. Il voit, il fait vivre, il vit ses personnages; ils semblent se mouvoir dans le milieu qui leur est naturel. Le paysage, quelque sommaire qu'il soit, participe à l'action. La mise en scène, la composition sont d'un art achevé dont la simplicité voulue redouble l'intensité. Jusque dans les moindres fragments de quelque vers, ces qualités apparaissent, d'autant plus frappantes. Sa vision première est toute plastique. Le tableau, le quadro, comme il disait, se compose de lui-même. Il se plaît aux brusques débuts, aux entrées immédiates, et cette allure soudaine, qui précipite en plein drame, prête aux gestes, aux paroles et aux sentiments qu'ils expriment toute la force, le charme saisissant de la vie.

A clear distinction is made between Chénier's use of *mètre*—'la disposition mesurée et variée des syllabes du vers'—and his handling of *rythme*—'la disposition des vers de la strophe'. Heredia sees Ronsard as the great inventor of *rythmes* while Chénier, much less original than Ronsard in that respect, is praised as an outstanding deployer of *métrique*. As he discusses these aspects of Chénier's versification, Heredia is led to analyse the virtues of the alexandrine, explaining its force and flexibility when it is handled by a master as great as Chénier—and, we cannot help but reflect, by a poet of Heredia's own talent and sensitive skill:

Avec l'hexamètre grec, l'alexandrin français est le plus sonore, le plus solide, le plus suave, le plus souple des instruments poétiques. Il est composé, ainsi que l'a dit Ronsard, de douze à treize syllabes, suivant qu'il est masculin ou féminin. Ce grand vers contient donc tous les vers, d'une à treize syllabes, et, au moyen de l'enjambement, il semble pouvoir se prolonger indéfiniment. Malgré cette élasticité que l'enjambement prête à la phrase poétique, l'alexandrin ne perd jamais sa structure, sa personnalité, grâce au temps fort de la césure, si mobile qu'elle soit, et surtout grâce au rappel de la rime qui, on le doit remarquer, même dans les vers féminins de treize syllabes, sonne toujours sur la douzième [. . .]

Ce vers d'apparence si drue et si simple, se plie aux plus savantes complexités du mètre. Il peut être coupé, varié. Les muettes particulières à notre langue l'allongent, le rendent plus respirable. Elles y mêlent, à l'éclatante netteté latine, une douceur fluide, une sorte de perspective, d'atmosphère vaporeuse.

Jamais poète n'a si magistralement manié l'alexandrin. Pour Chénier, le métal solide qui le constitue est aussi ductile que la glaise, aussi malléable que la cire sous les doigts du sculpteur. Il le pétrit, il le brise, il le renoue à son gré. On dirait qu'il le modèle. Le vers obéissant semble suivre la pensée, l'oreille, la vision du poète. Il l'étire, le ramasse ou l'arrête. Il en a si bien varié les coupes, que je doute qu'on en ait inventé depuis, qu'il n'eût essayées. Il se joue de l'immobile césure; il est plein de ternaires, de bi-césurés. A la fois instinctif et raffiné, il fait tenir en quelques syllabes des juxtapositions inattendues, des interversions d'une étrangeté charmante. Le premier, il a su opposer à la symétrie du mètre le prestigieux contraste de l'image [. . .] André Chénier fut donc, en syntaxe aussi bien qu'en métrique, un novateur d'une audace extrême et certes plus outré que les plus fougueux romantiques. La violence, l'ardeur spontanées de son génie expliquent ces bizarreries, ces témérités volontaires.

The praise of the alexandrine as handled by Chénier and the belief that it is in itself powerful and flexible enough to cater for almost all the needs of any French poet would lead us to expect from the mature Heredia a conservative attitude to new poetic movements. This is exactly the case when he speaks at length of Symbolist poetry to Georges Le Cardonnel and Charles Vellay[2] in 1905, which, we have noted, was the year of his death as well as the year when 'Le Manuscrit des *Bucoliques*' was published. He remains scrupulously polite, acknowledges with obvious sincerity the interest of the innovations attempted by poets like Verhaeren, Régnier, Kahn and Vielé-Griffin and praises the talent shown by such poets. But he is fundamentally un-receptive to these new inspirations and sees their alleged novelty as little more than a return to the Middle Ages or as a rather naïve refurbishing of old procedures. The so-called *vers libre* receives short shrift. The most one can say is that the Symbolists have increased the freedom of poets with regard to the use of hiatus and the mobility of the caesura. Hiatus, he affirms, is a question of personal taste. Some cases are harmonious and others are unsuccessful, and modern young poets are producing some frightful hiatus. As regards the young poets' fondness for placing the caesura in the middle of a word, it has all been done before—witness Théodore de Banville:

Il y a donc des cas où la césure au milieu d'un mot peut produire un effet excellent. Le vers ternaire et le vers bi-césuré sont très souvent agréables. Mais actuellement les jeunes poètes font des séries de vers ternaires, ce qui est aussi fatigant que la monotonie des vers classiques.

To the question: 'Le vers libre, lui-même, vous paraît-il être quelque chose de vraiment nouveau, et de durable?' Heredia's reply is categorical: 'Non. On ne peut sortir de la tradition française'. He points out that the *vers libre* has existed for a very long time; it can be found in Quinault, Molière and La Fontaine. All the Symbolists have done is to dislocate it further:

Chez eux, écrire des vers libres, c'est, semble-t-il, écrire, et *considérer comme définitifs*, des vers en formation, des embryons de vers, pour ainsi dire. J'ai été frappé, en parcourant les manuscrits d'André Chénier, de trouver, parmi ces ébauches informes, des morceaux qui pourraient servir de modèles à ceux de nos jeunes poètes qui font des vers libres.

We therefore conclude that there is in the new Symbolist poetry a quite different conception of poetry's nature and function, an implied valuation of improvisation and so-called spontaneity which is necessarily rejected by a poet like Heredia whose ideal always entails the careful creation of a perfected verbal structure as far removed as possible from the partial standpoint of one man. The *vers libre*

n'est pas autre chose qu'un artifice typographique qui permet de pousser le rythme au delà de l'alexandrin, qui est sa mesure naturelle. Avec l'alexandrin, on peut, au moyen de l'enjambement, faire des vers de quatorze, quinze et même vingt-huit pieds, dans lesquels il y aura des repos à la césure et à la rime. L'alexandrin restera, croyez-moi, le vrai vers français.

He was not a good prophet.

The same conservatism, though perhaps even stronger, informs his views on the Symbolists' use of rhyme. He thinks they are definitely mistaken. 'Ils font des vers assonancés. C'est retourner aux chansons populaires, où l'assonance est excellente. C'est revenir à l'enfance de l'art, à un véritable balbutiement.' He concedes that rhyme is a convention, but an admirable one and one that is now essential, having emerged only after many generations of experiment. He dismisses as naïve the claim that the rules of rhyme inhibit poetic creation. On the contrary, rhyme imposes 'une obligation de recherche, de travail, de perfection'. The constraint of rhyme will often lead the really gifted poet to find new words and therefore new ideas that would not have occurred to him without that constraint. And Heredia brings forward the traditional argument that French needs rhyme because it is a less sonorous language than Spanish or Italian; in the latter languages, final syllables are strong, all the words rhyme with each other and the result is monotony and assonance. French, however, has minor sonorities, like the mute *e*. That is why rhyme is indispensable in French poetry: 'elle renforce la sonorité terminale du vers, le rappel du son'. The mute *e* gives French its gentleness and fluidity. It would be impossible to suppress it. A long series of lines of poetry without mute *e*s would be unbearable. With his sense of history and tradition, Heredia recalls that a poet as early as Ronsard felt the need to intermingle masculine with feminine rhymes. Regarding the liberties taken with rhyme by the new poets, it is amusing to see the fastidious academician expressing his marked distaste for rhyming the singular with the plural, e.g. *ils s'aiment* with *moi-même*. It is most instructive to note that, in any case, he prefers the singular to the plural (in this at least like the great Mallarmé). He shows his universalist leanings when he affirms that

l'emploi fréquent du pluriel est regrettable. La plupart du temps, le pluriel contient moins de choses que le singulier, parce que le singulier est plus indéterminé que le pluriel. *Le chêne* veut dire davantage que *les chênes*, *l'homme* que *les hommes*.

It is also significant that in this interview with Le Cardonnel and Vellay Heredia does not even begin to consider the *fond* of the new poetry, what some would see as its more or less metaphysical background, or the broader context in which contemporary poets are attempting to capture or suggest the mysterious or the ineffable. About the importance of music for modern poets Heredia does have something to say, referring to 'l'influence de Wagner, de cette sorte de mysticisme musical qu'est la musique de Wagner'. His opinion of this matter is firm, crisply given and quite inadequate in his failure to explain what is meant by the influence of the great German composer. Heredia remains a prisoner of Parnassian ideals, his mind closed to the interpenetration of the arts that Walter Pater wrote about so eloquently in England and that inspired many poets in France from Verlaine to Merrill and Kahn:

Ce qu'on peut donc reprocher aux symbolistes c'est d'avoir voulu introduire dans un art les procédés d'un autre art, d'avoir voulu orchestrer le vers français. C'est une erreur, car le vers a une musique qui lui est tout à fait spéciale et qui n'a aucun rapport avec celle des musiciens. D'ailleurs, la poésie contient la musique, car elle comprend tous les arts, et c'est ce qui en fait l'art suprême.

This confidence of the poet in his own art is splendid and we appreciate that Heredia's sonnets can have their own kind of 'music'. But it does not surprise us to learn from his daughter Marie, viz. Gérard d'Houville, that her father 'chantait faux, et toujours le même air'.[3] He seems quite simply not to have had much liking for music or appreciation of it.[4] Yet his theorizing about poetry makes him appear more confined to Parnassian standards than his quite catholic taste would lead us to suppose that he in fact was. Thus, several years after his death, his son-in-law Henri de Régnier recalled how Heredia delighted in reading aloud the poems of Baudelaire—such as 'Le Balcon' or 'Don Juan aux enfers'—

dont il admirait éloquemment la concision hardie ou la subtile souplesse. Il aimait le vers baudelairien pour son ossature élégante et forte. Il en vantait la convenance et l'ingéniosité verbales toujours en rapport avec la complication ou la gravité des pensées; il en prisait la riche coloration, les sonorités profondes, le contournement ou la carrure, le bloc solide ou l'arabesque délicate, l'art magicien, la sorcellerie.[5]

With this informed taste many of us would have the greatest sympathy but we note that there is no involvement by Heredia in Baudelaire's ideas or outlook as such: it is as an artist and from a predominantly aesthetic viewpoint that Heredia appreciates Baudelaire.

Since he is clearly unsympathetic to some of the directions that new poetry, however tentatively, is taking, it is when Heredia speaks of those earlier nineteenth-century poets for whom he has a positive admiration that his criteria become most clear. He rejects what are for him facile, partisan contrasts between poets of different persuasions. He thus declines any stereotyped oppositions between Hugo and Lamartine. He sees them as individual and incomparable, loves them both and synthesizes the two in his all-embracing preoccupations of a practitioner of poetry, while pinpointing their specific qualities:

Victor Hugo est, au sens antique, le Poète, le faiseur de vers par excellence. C'est le maître du verbe et des images qu'il suscite. Il sait tous les mots de la langue, leur pouvoir virtuel, le sens mystérieux de leurs relations et quels éclats inattendus, quels sons inouïs il en peut tirer. Prodigieux visionnaire, sa puissance objective est telle qu'il matérialise l'idée. Il fait toucher l'impalpable, il fait voir l'invisible. Il a trouvé des couleurs pour peindre l'ombre et des images pour figurer le néant. Cet artiste souverain a connu tous les secrets de l'art et nous les a transmis. Nous les lui devons tous. Lamartine, au contraire, déconcerte l'analyse par une simplicité divine. D'ailleurs, qu'importe? Quelle qu'en soit la façon, 'Le Lac' et 'Le Crucifix' ne sont-ils pas les plus beaux chants d'amour qu'aient inspirés à l'homme éphémère l'éternité de la nature et le désir de l'immortalité?[6]

The last words of the quotation give us a glimpse of an assumption often explicit in Heredia's comments about other poets, that man's nature is unchanging, that he is the same in 1895 as he was in the time of Plato or Horace. This classical view partly explains why Heredia avoids overt personal intrusion in either his prose or his poetry:

Ces confessions publiques, menteuses ou sincères, révoltent en nous une pudeur profonde. Seul le génie a le droit de tout dire. Et pourtant, ce n'est qu'en les généralisant par une idéalisation naturelle ou volontaire, que les poètes ont pu, sans paraître impertinents, expliquer leurs sentiments intimes. Lamartine en est le plus admirable exemple. C'est que la vraie poésie est dans la nature et dans l'humanité éternelles et non dans le cœur de l'homme d'un jour, quelque grand qu'il soit. Elle est essentiellement simple, antique, primitive et, pour cela, vénérable. Depuis Homère, elle n'a rien inventé, hormis quelques images neuves pour peindre ce qui a toujours été. Le poète est d'autant plus vraiment et largement humain qu'il est plus impersonnel.[7]

In 1894, Leconte de Lisle is praised for the same capacity to give an impersonal, universalized evocation of man's eternal nature. The apparent distinction between *l'âme antique* and *l'âme moderne* is gathered up in the unifying concept of *l'Humanité*:

Puissant évocateur, il a suscité devant nous les dieux, les races, les civilisations disparus, les bêtes sauvages, les pays lointains. En des vers d'une beauté sereine ou tragique, il a traduit le tumulte des passions, l'éternel désir, l'horreur et l'attrait de la mort, les révoltes de la raison ou de l'orgueil, l'angoisse du désespoir, ce que l'amour et la foi ont de plus féroce et de plus suave, toute l'âme antique, toute l'âme moderne, l'Humanité. Tel fut cet impassible.[8]

It is not just poets who are seen in this classical perspective. In his preface in 1895 to a book of illustrations by the gifted artist Daniel Vierge who did the illustrations for the poet's translation, *La Nonne Alferez*, Heredia's viewpoint is again synthetic and universal:

Depuis les premiers jours du monde, l'homme, toujours le même, mû par les mêmes passions atroces, viles ou sublimes, s'agite dans la nature immuable. Divers par la race, il est semblable par les instincts.⁹

In his concluding remarks of 'Le Manuscrit des *Bucoliques*', he affirms that

la matière poétique est, à vrai dire, éternellement la même; ce n'est que par l'invention d'images neuves que les poètes, de siècle en siècle, la renouvellent et la diversifient. Mais seule, la forme parfaite d'une œuvre peut en perpétuer la gloire.¹⁰

This view of human nature and these universalizing tendencies admired and exemplified by Heredia account for much in his poetry and prose and particularly for the fact that he takes it for granted that there is nothing much that is really new to say about man or life: for an artist so strongly influenced by the past, by Greek and Roman culture as much as by the Renaissance, there is not much new that any artist can say. When new poetry is read and assessed, it is the versification, the manner, style and form which merit attention. For Gautier and the Parnassians, we recall, form was not easily distinguishable from content. In a letter accompanying the publication of Philippe Dufour's *Poèmes légendaires* (Lemerre, 1897), Heredia recalls how he and Dufour first met at Leconte de Lisle's salon and how, when Dufour had left, the Master praised one of Dufour's poems: 'Lisez ce poème, fit-il, les vers en sont solidement construits.' Regretting that Leconte de Lisle did not live long enough to present Dufour's poems, Heredia adopts the same criteria:

Mais l'œuvre [Leconte de Lisle's] survit à l'homme, son souvenir vénéré subsiste, sa doctrine demeure. Vous m'avez fait l'honneur de me choisir pour parler en son nom, et ce n'est qu'en me prévalant de son autorité que j'ose recommander vos vers à ceux qui se plaisent encore aux pensées graves, à la cadence des beaux rhythmes, à la belle sonorité des rimes.

Oui, certes, ainsi que l'affirmait le grand poète, vos vers sont solides. Telle en est la qualité profonde.¹¹

French artists have a greater inclination to generalize than English ones, particularly about art and the artist's role. Heredia, born Spanish, became more French than the French and generalized frequently: he is at home with a kind of eloquence and even rhetoric that have become very suspect in many spheres of literature in the twentieth century. It may be difficult to derive precise details from such generalizations but as, from time to time, he surveys the role of the artist, poet, painter, illustrator or sculptor, we detect a characteristically impersonal affirmation of his own values. His traditional attachment to classical canons, his scorn for the values of Everyman and for what in his eyes is the brash superficiality of some modern tastes, his pride in the search for perfection which marked his own art and his concern for quality over quantity are all illustrated by the following conclusion to an article he wrote in 1886 on the sculptor Ernest Christophe:

L'œuvre de l'artiste dont nous venons de dire brièvement la vie, n'est pas nombreuse; mais elle n'a assurément rien de banal. Dans ce temps d'exhibitions à outrance où la notoriété d'un jour passe aisément pour de la gloire, il lui faut rendre cette haute justice qu'il n'a jamais flatté le goût du vulgaire et qu'il a préféré, par un orgueilleux respect de soi-même et de son art, l'approbation de quelques-uns à l'applaudisse-ment de tous.

On a reproché à Ernest Christophe la recherche philosophique de ses conceptions, son goût littéraire, la lenteur de sa production. Ces re-proches nous touchent peu. L'artiste, peintre, sculpteur ou poète, est le maître de choisir son sujet. Il ne relève que de sa volonté ou de son caprice. La critique doit se borner à juger l'œuvre qui, bonne, absout et glorifie l'auteur; mauvaise, le condamne. Un long et courageux effort vers la perfection rêvée impose le respect. Ce n'est pas le nombre des ouvrages, mais leur beauté, qui importe; et c'est le fait du génie in-conscient ou d'un esprit médiocre que de se contenter facilement.[12]

THE TRANSLATIONS

Of the three translations Heredia published, *La Nonne Alferez* (Lemerre, 1894) was his version of *La Monja Alferez* (*The Nun Ensign*, an ensign being a standard-bearer), the account, allegedly by herself, of the strange life of a nun, Catalina de Erauso, and her peregrinations, dressed as a swashbuckling gentleman in South America, especially Peru and Chile. Heredia was clearly drawn by the exotic interest, however superficial, generated by this picaresque account of morals and manners in South America during the early part of the seventeenth century; frequent adventures, simple action, fast narration, an uncluttered line, these are the essential traits of Heredia's accurate and excellent translation. The language and syntax of the original Spanish are mostly so straightforward that his talents could not have been greatly exercised. In the limited space we can afford to devote to Heredia's translations, it will be worth our while to concentrate our attention on the more taxing and rewarding tasks he undertook when he turned into French the Spanish of Bernal Díaz del Castillo and of Fernan Caballero.

The *Historia Verdadera de la Conquista de la Nueva España* was written by Bernal Díaz del Castillo, who was born in Spain at Medina del Campo in 1492, the year in which Columbus discovered the New World, and died in Guatemala at the age of about eighty-nine. Following Pedro Arias de Avila to the New World in 1514, he had served as a soldier in the armada under Francisco Hernandez de Cordoba which, in 1517, discovered the Yucatan peninsula, then in the second expedition led by Juan de Grijalva which, in 1518, explored the coast west of the Yucatan peninsula but above all, he had served in the expedition under Hernando Cortés that set sail in 1519 on a journey that was to lead to the conquest of Mexico, Guatemala, Honduras and Nicaragua. Díaz was over seventy when he began writing his account. He gave it up for a time, discouraged by his comparison between his own unpolished language and the more accomplished literary style of other historians treating the same subject like Francisco López de Gómara and Gonzalo de Illescas. But these two had much less first-hand knowledge of the campaigns in New Spain than Díaz himself, who had served and fought in many of them. Irritated and angered by their inaccuracies and misrepresentations—to the point that his narrative is often interrupted by sharp criticisms of both, especially Gómara—he resumed and completed his writing in his late seventies. The recognition of his account as a historical document of the highest importance had begun long before Heredia's day but that such recognition has increased is shown by the attention Díaz has received in more recent times.[13]

Heredia's decision to translate Díaz could not have been lightly taken: it was to involve him in some fifteen years of work, not the least of which was the reading and research required. The four volumes of the *Véridique Histoire de la conquête de la Nouvelle Espagne* (Lemerre, 1877, 1879, 1881, 1887) cover 1450 pages as well as over 150 pages of notes and appendices. The most obvious reason for Heredia's sustained interest in Díaz was that the *Véridique Histoire* concerned the part of the world from which Heredia himself had sprung and where his Spanish ancestors had settled in the century that saw Cortés achieve his spectacular conquests. The Caribbean was in his blood and folk memory. He had been born and brought up in the island of Cuba from which the armada set sail to found Vera Cruz and take Mexico.

Another reason for Heredia's involvement in the *Véridique Histoire* was undoubtedly the attraction of the subject. Personal interest and ancestral pride joined with the powerful appeal of such an epic, heroic and exotic account of the clash between two civilizations, Spanish and Aztec. The armada that left Santiago de Cuba under Cortés numbered eleven ships and some three hundred soldiers. They were to receive some limited reinforcement from time to time before their eventual conquest of Mexico but the odds against them were almost unbelievably heavy: hundreds of thousands of Mexicans and other Indians, harsh terrain that with its mountains, forests, heat and mosquitoes was brutally taxing, limited supplies of food, weapons and powder. The Spaniards never doubted their own beliefs and values. For the twentieth-century reader, their notion of friendship extended to the Indians can be bizarre in its unconscious humour, as in chapter 66, when Díaz gives us his account of how Cortés, after a savage battle with the people of Tlascala, then tried to establish good relations by ordering them

de venir aussitôt appointer la paix et nous donner passage, par leur terre, pour aller à Mexico, comme nous leur avions déjà fait dire: que, s'ils ne venaient traiter immédiatement, nous leur tuerions tous leurs gens, et que, les aimant beaucoup et désirant les avoir pour frères, nous n'aurions jamais voulu les outrager en rien, s'ils ne nous en avaient pas donné motif. Cortès ajouta quantité de flatteries pour les attirer à notre amitié.

The character of Cortés fascinated Heredia, as he explicitly demonstrates in his introduction (i, pp. li-lxiii). Cortés was intensely loyal to the Spanish crown and to the Catholic church. Each area he conquered was annexed to the Spanish emperor Charles V and, if possible, brought immediately into Christendom: with the different values born of the pluralistic societies in which we live, we note with bemused interest that the attendant priest and lawyer ensured that the proper legal and ecclesiastical forms were followed. Cortés's sincere and prompt concern was to stop the local barbarous human sacrifices to the Mexican gods, the cannibalism and the sodomy he was shocked to discover. His personal courage is revealed by many hand-to-hand encounters. He was an astute military commander and an even astuter politician in his dealings both with his own troops and with the natives. Towards the former he was firm and outwardly fair, always conscious of their interests and welfare and regularly taking soundings of their opinions. With the natives he played a double game, preventing his Spanish soldiers and his gradually acquired native troops from pillaging in order to persuade further *pueblos* and tribes to abandon their abject subjection to Mexico's savage rule and pay homage to the just, beneficent Spaniards, while using every trick he could to discredit the Mexican emperor Montezuma, show him as weak and powerless and demonstrate the superhuman qualities of the Spaniards. In this desire Cortés was aided by chance. The Spanish horses created panic because they were unknown in the New World and at first the Mexicans thought a horse and its Spanish rider formed a kind of prodigious fighting centaur. The Spanish canons were cunningly projected as magical powers. Above all, Cortés exploited to the full Montezuma's belief that the Spaniards were the *Teules*, gods or demons of a new race come from the East who, according to Mexican belief, would conquer the earth. If his resolution had been firm, Montezuma could have wiped out the small force of Spaniards with all their intelligence, bravery and superior weapons. Instead, the Mexican emperor wavered, now sending his troops or subservient tribes to attack Cortés, now sending him presents of gold and cloth, despatching envoys to tell him he must not come to Mexico but yielding step by step to the ever urbane insistence transmitted by Cortés through returning envoys that he must come to Mexico to pay his respects to the great Mexican emperor. Using every adventitious resource at their command,

Cortés and his men actually walk into Mexico city to be greeted by a welcoming Montezuma in all his glory. Once resident in the capital, Cortés simply seizes Montezuma and, while treating him with due respect, makes him prisoner in one of his own palaces. It is only later that the Mexicans rebel and with savage fighting oust the Spaniards who have to wage intensely fierce and bloody battles to win control of the city, aided by thousands of natives who have by then learned to be loyal to the great Cortés. Heredia's summary portrait of the great *conquistador* is well drawn:

Du jour que l'occasion lui est offerte, le Héros apparaît, politique plus encore que guerrier. Il ne s'embarrasse point de scrupules vulgaires. Il sait brusquer les volontés, mûrir vite un plan, précipiter une résolution. Le génie de Cortès est d'une trempe rare. Il a l'éclat froid, la souplesse, la rigidité, le ressort d'une bonne lame. Il plie aisément. Il se redresse sans effort. Moins sublime que Colomb, plus heureux et non moins grand que Balboa, Cortès eut la faculté suprême qui manqua toujours à son rival, le grossier Pizarre: il sut grandir avec sa fortune (i, p. lxiii).

But as much as by the figure of Cortés and the epic nature of the *Véridique Histoire*, Heredia was drawn by the qualities of the narrative. He explains in his *avertissement* (i, pp. i-iii) how his enthusiasm for his subject grew:

Né dans un temps fertile en prodiges, Bernal Díaz fut un témoin actif. Il a tracé d'une main naïve et rude le tableau de la grande aventure mexicaine. Nous en donnons au public français une copie exacte.

A mesure que nous traduisions cette chronique et que nous recherchions dans les historiens contemporains des documents propres à éclaircir le texte, nous nous prenions pour notre sujet d'un intérêt grandissant. De cette longue intimité avec l'aventurier héroïque est sortie une œuvre nouvelle. Nous avons voulu le faire revivre. Nous avons tenté de peindre, autour de lui, l'Espagne aux premières années du XVIe siècle, tout un peuple halluciné, la croisade cupide qui le précipita vers l'Amérique, une nature vierge, la civilisation brillante et barbare des Aztèques, l'écroulement de leur vaste empire.

Bernal Díaz wrote with the conviction that he had taken part in one of the most glorious enterprises of all time and that it had been successful and he had survived only through the divine protection of the Virgin Mary and his Lord Jesus Christ. I have recalled that he realized he could not command the literary elegance of a Gómara. In fact, that he could not do so was really an advantage: his burning sincerity, his overriding concern for accuracy and his personal involvement give his account superb authority and directness. Veracity and justice—to all the *conquistadores* and not just to Cortés—are what concern Díaz as he evokes the details of every encounter from the cape of Cotoche, on the eastern side of the Yucatan peninsula, to the splendours and anguish of the Mexican campaign and the rigorous overland journey to Honduras. He clearly enjoyed a good fight and it is with a fierce relish that he regularly recounts the 'bonnes estocades et taillades' ('buenas estocadas y cuchilladas') that he and his companions delivered in hand-to-hand fighting during the wars fought at Champoton, Tabasco, Cingapacenga, Tlascala or, most of all, during the ninety-three days and nights it took Cortés and his men to recapture Mexico city with the help of the ships he had had specially built to strengthen his capacity for naval warfare on the lagoon on which the city was built. Díaz recaptures the harsh exoticism of the Aztec civilization where the names alone play their part, like those of the *Caciques* or chiefs from Tlascala: Masse-Escaci, Xicotenga, Guaxocingo, Chichime-catecle, Tecapaneca de Topeyanco (chapter 74). The description of the first and peaceful entry into Mexico on 8 November 1519 (chapter 88) conveys the awe of the Spaniards as they survey the riches and commerce of the Aztec capital and the variety of goods and manufactures sold in Mexico's enormous central square, the *Tatelulco*. Perhaps most impressively exotic of all is the evocation of the main temple with its huge statues of the two principal Aztec deities, Huichilobos, their god of war, and Tezcatepuca, god of hell, with their horrible viperine ornaments and the pervading stench of blood from human sacrifices. The Aztecs ripped out the hearts of their victims (such as Spaniards when caught, more normally captured enemies from the region or slaves bred specially to be sacrificed), chopped off their arms and legs which were cooked and eaten and threw the remains of the bodies to the animals and birds of prey kept for that purpose. Díaz gives systematically detailed accounts of all the various aspects of the Mexican capital. But he also sets the struggles in Mexico in the larger context of events back home in Spain and in the islands of Hispaniola and Cuba. To the formidable difficulties encountered by Cortés on the ground were added the treacherous plots of Diego Velasquez, the governor of Cuba who had initially launched Cortés on his expedition and of Juan Rodriguez de Fonseca, bishop of Burgos and President of the Royal Council of the Indies who was influential at the Spanish court until his selfish dealings were later laid bare and he was dismissed. Diego Velasquez sought to revoke Cortés's appointment by sending other troops from Cuba to New Spain. Cortés outwitted them all.

Díaz's sense of justice and humanity ensures that his history remains lively and interesting. He is too fiercely independent not sometimes to criticize Cortés. While regularly acknowledging his greatness as soldier and leader, he notes that Cortés did not share out equally the gold they captured, taking, in addition to the royal fifth for the Spanish crown, another fifth for himself and other amounts unspecified. It was Cortés who at Vera Cruz had the idea of destroying the ships that had brought the *conquistadores* there so that, with no possibility of return to Cuba, resolve to conquer would thereby be hardened among his soldiers; but he waited for this idea to come from his men so that, Díaz notes, if the cost of the ships had to be repaid, Cortés could argue that the idea had originated from them all and all would have to pay (chapter 53). Far from idealizing Cortés, Díaz can remark, after explaining the involved dealings concerning Montezuma's treasure, that 'Cortès, sous couleur de justice impartiale, n'était qu'un grand artisan de ruses' (chapter 106). But Díaz's humanity comes out most markedly in occasional personal asides as when, in chapter 16, he plants six or eight orange pips he had brought from Cuba ('J'ai remémoré ici ce fait pour que l'on sache que ce furent les premiers orangers plantés dans la Nouvelle Espagne') or when, in chapter 41, he writes: 'Et je dis à mon compagnon de rester au poste et que j'irais avec eux [some Indians, enemies of Montezuma], car en cette saison, les pieds ne me pesaient pas comme à présent que je suis vieux'. His predominant concern with veracity leads to many detailed descriptions of battles, casualties and incidents, inevitably entailing at times a measure of repetitiveness, but the same veracity can cast interesting light on the poignantly complex plights into which some Spaniards were thrown. Thus in chapter 27 we read of the attempt by Ordas, sent by Cortés, to rescue two Spaniards from an earlier expedition who have been kept prisoner by the natives on the east coast of Yucatan, near the cape of Cotoche. One of these prisoners, Gonzalo Guerréro, has married an Indian woman, now has three sons and unlike the other Spaniard, Gerónimo de Aguilar, does not want to rejoin his countrymen. The human situation is cogently dramatized by Díaz's dialogue:

Frère Aguilar, je suis marié, j'ai trois fils et on me tient ici pour Cacique [chief or leader] et Capitaine en temps de guerre. Allez avec Dieu; pour moi j'ai la figure tatouée et les oreilles percées. Que diraient de moi ces Espagnols, s'ils me voyaient ainsi accommodé? Et puis voyez ces trois miens petits enfants: qu'ils sont jolis! Par votre vie, donnez-moi de ces grains de verroterie verte [glass beads] que vous apportez et je dirai que mes frères me les envoient de mon pays. Et mêmement, l'Indienne, femme de Gonzalo, apostropha l'Aguilar et lui dit, fort en colère, en son langage: Voyez donc un peu cet esclave qui vient appeler mon mari! Allez-vous-en, vous, et ne vous mêlez point de bavarder davantage.—Et l'Aguilar recommença à parler au Gonzalo, lui remontrant qu'il était chrétien, et qu'il ne perdît point son âme pour une Indienne, et que s'il les tenait pour sa femme et ses enfants, qu'il les emmenât avec lui, puisqu'il ne les voulait pas laisser. Et pour chose qu'il lui pût dire et pour bien qu'il l'admonestât, l'homme ne voulut point venir.

A comparison between Heredia's translation and the Spanish text he used shows that he contrived both to follow it closely and faithfully and also to breathe into it just as much life as is found in Díaz. The biggest challenge Heredia set himself was self-imposed, to capture as much as he could of the style of sixteenth-century French while ensuring that his version was intelligible to the contemporary reader. Flaubert and Leconte de Lisle were two of his friends who took particular delight in the subject and style of the *Véridique Histoire*. Leconte de Lisle's assessment of the first volume was high indeed:

Tous ceux qui ont un vrai sens littéraire applaudiront votre belle introduction et la solide langue semi-archaïque que vous avez inventée au plus grand profit du vieux chroniqueur. J'ai tout lu ligne par ligne, ayant parfaitement oublié que je lisais une traduction, ce qui est le meilleur compliment que je puisse vous faire (cf. Ibrovac, i, p. 140).

The flavour of Heredia's prose can be properly tasted only by

reading his translation. While sometimes modifying the original punctuation for greater effect and clarity, his main aim was to introduce archaic syntax and vocabulary of many different kinds, like *souventes fois* (often), *vitement* (vite), *trucheman* (interpreter), *le jour ensuivant* (the next day), *sur la mi-nuit* (at midnight), *oncques* (never), *occire* (to kill), *navrer* (to wound), *souler* (to have the habit of), *issir* (to go out). The result is sentences like the following, perfectly understandable to a modern reader but conveying the impression of a chronicle belonging to a distant age. 'Et de tout ce nous nous émerveillâmes grandement comme de chose oncques vue ni ouïe' (chapter 3): 'Cortès fut marri de sa fuite, craignant qu'il ne dît aux Indiens ses compatriotes quelque chose qui nous préjudiciât' (chapter 32): 'La première chose qu'ils firent fut de publier contre nous la guerre à feu et à sang et à tout pillage franc' (chapter 121): 'Et incontinent [immediately], l'aventure fut sue de tout le camp' (chapter 144): 'Et malgré qu'ils nous fissent si grief dommage, ce nonobstant nous boutâmes outre par la chaussée, jusqu'à un pont' (chapter 150): 'force escadrons nous vinrent sus' (chapter 151): En ces rencontres, force Mexicains furent également occis ou navrés' (chapter 151).

When due allowance has been made for Heredia's success in archaizing the French of the *Véridique Histoire*, we recognize that his greatest achievement was to capture the whole sweep of its spirit of dogged courage, remorseless endeavour and hunger for gold as well as to rise to the simple dignity of feeling and expression required at key moments such as the consideration of naïve wonderment and careful observation of detail at the first sight of the great Montezuma amid what seemed to the *conquistadores* the dream-like splendours of the mighty city of Mexico:

Nous approchions de Mexico. A un endroit où il y a des petites tours, le grand Montezuma descendit de litière. Les grands Caciques le soutenaient par les bras, sous un dais riche à merveille, tissu de plumes de couleur verte, tout ouvragé d'or, d'argent, de perles et de pierres chalchihuites qui pendaient en franges. Et le grand Montezuma s'avançait, très-splendidement accoutré à sa façon. Il avait aux pieds des cutaras, ainsi nomment-ils leur chaussure, couvertes de riches pierreries, et dont les semelles étaient d'or. Les quatre seigneurs qui lui soutenaient les bras, portaient de somptueux vêtements, à leur mode. On les leur avait probablement préparés sur la route, pour escorter leur seigneur,

car ce n'était pas les mêmes habits qu'ils avaient lorsqu'ils vinrent nous recevoir. A côté d'eux, tenant le dais sur leurs têtes, marchaient d'autres puissants Caciques. Plusieurs seigneurs précédaient le grand Montezuma, balayant le sol où il devait passer et y étendant des mantes, de peur qu'il ne foulât la terre. Aucun de ces seigneurs n'osait, même en pensée, le regarder au visage. Ils allaient tous, les yeux baissés, avec un profond respect, hormis ses quatre parents et neveux qui le tenaient par le bras (chapter 88).

This resurrection of the past was in the best tradition of the Parnassian movement and accomplished with the express approval and encouragement of Leconte de Lisle. Yet it was at the same time very original, being concerned not with Greece or Rome of two thousand years ago but with the New World in the sixteenth century. The two studies in the introduction to the first volume—'Espagne 1513-14' and 'la Jeunesse de Cortès'— are tersely, vividly executed and quite original compositions serving to situate the reader in the times. On pp. lxv-lxvii of his first volume Heredia with conscientious erudition lists the thirteen volumes he has had occasion to quote in his two preliminary studies. The notes at the end of each volume of his translation, while avoiding any vain parade of esoteric knowledge, help us to understand particular terms and names of places that would understandably be alien to most of us as well as linking various points made by Díaz with writers ancient and modern. As he explains in his 'Notes et Eclaircissements' (iv, p. 253), the manuscript on which Heredia based his translation was the one in Spain that had been used by Father Alonso Remón in his edition (Madrid, 1632). By the end of his fourth and last volume (Appendix: 'Le Manuscrit de la Véridique Histoire', pp. 401-5), Heredia has discovered that the original manuscript lies in Guatemala. His account of how he made this discovery is strangely hurried and unclear:

Guidé par une intuition passionnée, aidé dans nos recherches par un intelligent ami, nous avons eu la fortune de retrouver intact, après trois cents ans, ce précieux et vénérable monument de la grande conquête. Où? Comment? Le récit en serait singulier. Le curieux lecteur nous excusera de ne le lui point faire. Le manuscrit n'est pas entre nos mains [. . .]

Heredia was thus not able to consult the original manuscript,[14]

though in the best manner of an *ancien chartiste* he gives a detailed description of it which his friend has sent him and includes at the beginning of this last volume of his translation a photograph copy of one page of Díaz's manuscript. He has learned enough of the original manuscript in Guatemala to realize that Remón made many changes, some large and many slight, mostly for reasons religious and political. Heredia thus based his translation on a text that had been adulterated by Remón as he transcribed from the one copy in Spain of the original manuscript in the library of Don Lorenzo Ramirez de Prado. But the changes made by Remón are not so great that they have significance for our purposes in this study or for those of us who want to read Heredia's translation. The punctuation, spelling and abbreviations of the original manuscript make it difficult to read by anyone in our time; in his changes in these respects Remón was in the seventeenth century only anticipating more recent scholars who are not so purist as to want to inflict on us Díaz's manuscript in every authentic detail. Heredia had made every scholarly endeavour to get to the original manuscript. His *pièces justificatives* at the end of his fourth volume complete his aim of historical accuracy, with his translation of the letters and other documents concerning Bernal Díaz, his father-in-law and younger son, published by D. Francisco-Antonio de Fuentes y Guzman (*Historia de Guatemala*, Madrid, Luis Navarro, 1882). With the publication of the fourth and last volume of the *Véridique Histoire*, Heredia had successfully concluded an enterprise that had made considerable demands on him as both scholar and artist.[15] By a curious twist of fate, when Heredia had finished the first volume of his translation in the year before it was actually published, there appeared another translation by someone who had been working quite independently of him (D. Jourdanet, Paris, Lahure, 1876, two volumes). When he received a complimentary copy of the other scholar's work, Heredia's comment was affably polite:

N'est-ce pas chose singulière que deux hommes d'étude se soient rencontrés après trois cents ans, sur une chronique oubliée? Il est à regretter que le remarquable travail de M. Jourdanet n'ait été imprimé qu'à un trop petit nombre d'exemplaires. Nous sommes heureux de partager avec un savant distingué l'honneur d'avoir, pour la première fois, traduit en français la *Véridique Histoire* du vieux Conquistador, Bernal Díaz del Castillo.

Juan Soldado was translated by Heredia from a book of popular Spanish stories collected together by Fernan Caballero.[16] It appeared in the *Journal des débats* on 1 January 1885. By far the shortest of Heredia's translations, it is also brilliantly comic. He described it as 'librement traduit d'un des *Cuentos populares* publiés par F. Caballero'. In fact, he kept fairly close to the original and his successful fusion of fantasy and joviality owed much to the Spanish version. The main liberties he took with the Spanish were to avoid a few expressions for which there is no suitable equivalent in French, to add phrases here and there to increase the comedy and to change the order of some impressions for better effect.

Juan is a soldier who, after twenty-four years of service in the army, has been paid off with six maravedis (old Spanish coins) and a pound of bread. This will become a refrain comically repeated many times during the story—'qui, après avoir servi vingt-quatre ans le roi, n'en a retiré qu'une livre de pain et six maravédis'. At the beginning, despite his poverty, Juan is full of courage and good cheer as he walks, singing, along the king's highway. His first encounter is with Christ who, with Saint Peter as his guide, 'courait le monde en quête d'âmes charitables et quémandait le long des chemins'. Heredia strengthens the comic touch here by his description of Saint Peter. 'Saint-Pierre qui, grâce à sa tête chauve et à sa longue barbe blanche, semblait plus apitoyant, lui demanda l'aumône.' Juan briefly but eloquently explains his situation, with the first repetition of his refrain, but willingly shares his bread between the three of them. A couple of leagues on, the two celestial beggars approach him again. 'Il me semble bien que je vous ai donné tout à l'heure et que je connais ce vieux chauve-là', observes Juan as he notes Saint Peter's bald pate. 'Bien que, après avoir servi vingt-quatre ans le roi, je n'aie qu'une livre de pain et six maravédis et que, de la livre de pain, il ne me reste que ce morceau, je le partagerai avec vous.' This he does and at once eats the bit of bread he then has left in case the two beggars ask again. The sun is setting when Jesus and Saint Peter accost him a third time. Same request, more good-humoured protest from Juan who barely has time to start his usual refrain before Saint Peter interrupts and takes it up for him, until Juan interjects: 'Ah! vieux malicieux, s'écria Juan Soldado en riant, puisque tu sais mieux que moi le compte de ma monnaie, tiens, prends!' He gives them four of his six maravedis and goes on his way remarking a little ruefully on the short distance between himself and starvation.

Saint Peter persuades Christ to do something for this poor devil of a soldier, 'qui, après avoir servi vingt-quatre ans le roi, n'en a retiré qu'une livre de pain et six maravédis qu'il a partagés avec nous'. At this point Heredia gives a mock dignity greater than in the Spanish original to Saint Peter who observes that Juan, 'quoiqu'un peu familier, fut charitable'. Juan is therefore told to ask for anything he wants. After careful thought, he requests and is granted the power to order anything he likes to enter his knapsack. The familiar fairytale fantasy of unlimited power through the repetition of one wish can now be developed. Passing through a village, Juan espies some lovely fat loaves of bread on a table and, hanging from the beams of the ceiling, some delicious sausages simply asking to be eaten. 'Au sac!', he cries. 'Et voilà les miches roulant comme roues, les andouilles se défilant avec des trémoussemens de couleuvres agiles, droit au sac.' Mine host of the inn and the cook's boy are described with comic verve chasing after the bread and the sausages. Juan normally went hungry and was used to having 'plus d'appétit que Dieu n'a de patience'; this day he had a glorious feast.

Night falls. Arriving at a small market-town, he goes to the town hall to collect a ticket entitling him, as a veteran, to a bed for the night. The alcalde offers him lodging in a nearby property which no one will go near because it is haunted by the ghost of its former owner, a dreadful miscreant and sinner who has recently died unconfessed. If Juan is a good Christian and a brave soldier, he will have no problem, says the alcalde: on the contrary, he will lodge well because the owner was very wealthy and the property abounds in good things. Nothing daunted, Juan willingly accepts the offer. 'Juan Soldado', he says, 'ne doit ni ne craint rien'— another little refrain ('Juan Soldado ni debe ni teme'). He takes up residence with full cellar and larder. In traditional picaresque fashion, he first fills a jug with wine—'car il estimait que sang d'ivrogne est trop chaud pour charrier la peur'—and starts to grill his *rillettes*. He has scarcely sat down when a cavernous voice rings down the chimney. 'Peut-on descendre?' ('Caigo?') To this polite if alarming enquiry Juan responds with the imperturbability of the canny soldier armed with liquid courage. 'Descend si ça te plaît, répondit Juan Soldado déjà tout allumé par les riches lampées de vin qu'il se coulait entre dos et poitrine.' And his two refrains come together. 'Celui qui a servi vingt-quatre ans le roi, sans en tirer autre chose qu'une livre de pain et six maravédis, ne craint ni ne doit rien'. A man's leg then falls down the chimney. Trembling and hair bristling, Juan takes a long swig of wine and tremulously asks if the gentleman ghost would like to be buried. The movement of one toe of the leg indicates no desire for burial. 'Alors, pourris-là', Juan vigorously concludes. In a few moments, the cavernous voice enquires again down the chimney. 'Peut-on descendre?' Same response from Juan or at least the beginning of the same response because Heredia heightens the comic effect by breaking off the repeating refrain with 'Le reste se perdit dans un glouglou'. Another leg falls down the chimney and there then follow all the various parts of the ghostly body which quickly put themselves together to reconstitute the former owner's full person. The ghost observes that Juan is a brave man. Yes, replies Juan, 'Jamais repu, toujours vaillant', that is his style. And he launches into his usual refrain. The ghost tells him to forget about his poverty and past hardships; if Juan will do as he is bid, his future will be secure and he will save the ghost's soul. Juan readily agrees to do as he is asked 'quand bien même il faudrait recoudre Votre Grâce pour l'empêcher de s'éparpiller'. The ghost notes that Juan seems to be drunk. 'Non, Monsieur, non, certes, tout au plus ému. Votre Grâce ne doit pas ignorer qu'il y a trois classes d'ivrognes: les gais, les gris et les saoûls. Je n'ai pas encore dépassé l'extrême gaieté.' The outcome is a visit to the cellar. The ghost tells Juan to dig. 'Creusez vous-même, si vous en avez envie, répondit Juan. Je n'ai pas servi vingt-quatre ans le roi sans en tirer autre profit qu'une livre de pain et six maravédis, pour reprendre du service sous un maître qui peut-être ne m'en donnera pas autant.' The ghost then digs up three jars, one full of sous which he asks Juan to give to the poor, the second of silver to be spent on prayers for the ghost's soul, the third of gold, for Juan himself when he has done as required. Juan complies, repeating his refrain with greater satisfaction than before and becomes 'Sa Seigneurerie Don Juan Soldado'.

Meanwhile, Lucifer is enraged at losing a damned soul through so much effective praying in church. He plots vengeance on Juan by enlisting the help of Satanasillo, the craftiest little devil in Hell. Lucifer promises Satanasillo various rewards—'un assortiment de rubans et de bijoux pour tenter et pervertir les filles d'Eve, et toutes les cartes et les outres de vin qu'il voudrait pour séduire et perdre les fils d'Adam'. Satanasillo drops in on Juan, who is taking the air in his garden. He greets Satanasillo with a mixture of politeness and jocularly insulting pleasantries. He offers the visitor a cigarette. The little devil smokes only sulphur. Perhaps he would take a glass of white sherry? Satanasillo drinks only nitric acid. When Juan grasps the fact that Lucifer's envoy has come for him, he goes for his knapsack and the familiar shout 'Au sac!' puts Satanasillo well and truly in the bag. Seizing a mallet, Juan then gives him a sound thrashing through the knapsack. The little devil crawls back to Hell 'rompu, éreinté' désossé,, informe'. Lucifer is furious, comically so with his imprecations ('par les cornes de la lune!'). He will himself deal with the upstart Juan Soldado. Juan is expecting him. He serenely warns the devil: 'Compère Lucifer, Juan Soldado ne craint ni ne doit rien. Il est bon que tu le saches'. Lucifer explodes in a shower of picturesque threats and insults, fire and smoke belching from his mouth. Juan threatens him with the knapsack. Lucifer extends his black arm and terrible claws. . . . 'Au sac!' cries Juan. 'Et Lucifer eut beau se tordre, se hérisser, se pelotonner, bramer, hurler, bouffer, fumer, tonner et pétarader, il lui fallut aller au sac'. And he gets a fiercer drubbing in it than the one awarded to Satanasillo. Juan then dismisses him with appropriate warnings of the fate that will befall him if he returns. The picture of Lucifer slinking back to Hell and of his reception there reaches a high point of hilarious exaggeration:

Lorsque dans sa cour infernale rentra le Grand Diable, la queue entre les jambes comme un chien battu, hagard, perclus, estropié, criblé, vanné, si transparent qu'on lui voyait la flamme à travers, toute la

Diablerie, vomissant crapauds et vipères, rugit en chœur : Qu'allons-nous faire, Maître ?

Years later, Juan senses the approach of death. Cheerfully, 'il boucla son sac et prit le chemin du ciel'. Saint Peter is waiting at the gates of Heaven. There is a brisk exchange of words, Saint Peter pointing out that it is not that easy to get into Heaven. What good works can Juan cite? 'Avoir servi vingt-quatre ans le roi, sans autre récompense qu'une livre de pain et six maravédis, n'est-ce point assez, au jugement de Votre Sainte Grâce ? répondit courtoisement Juan Soldado.' Saint Peter makes it clear that it isn't enough. Juan expresses astonishment. 'Nous allons bien voir !' he replies, moving towards the heavenly gates, only to be stopped by Saint Peter. The inevitable 'Au sac !' rings out and Saint Peter is soon in the bag like the others, begging for mercy from dear Juan, his 'bon ami', his 'estimable ami'. This won't do at all, he pleads. The gates of Heaven are open with no porter : 'il y peut entrer n'importe quelle âme de nigaud' . . . 'C'est précisément mon cas ! conclut Juan Soldado faisant son entrée triomphale en Paradis, avec Saint Pierre sur le dos—N'ai-je pas, là-bas, servi vingt-quatre ans le roi sans autre profit qu'une livre de pain et six maravédis ?'

This tale is a gem in the original Spanish. The comically exaggerated absurdity of *Juan Soldado*, the serene good temper, cheeky opportunism and warm-heartedness of the hero and the traditional digs at reverence, religion and mankind generally are well conveyed by Heredia. He admirably captures the story's spirit and deploys his skill as a translator so well that the French version is even better than the Spanish. No reader of *Les Trophées* could surely have guessed that Heredia would have had either the inclination or the ability to take on a story of this sort. The only sonnet in the collection that might give us a hint of his obvious relish for comic effect is perhaps 'Hortorum Deus III' ('Rome et les Barbares'). It would be foolish to make too much of the translation of one story, of what is not much more than a trifle. We may nevertheless regret that Heredia did not fulfil his ambition to translate into French the *Don Quixote* of Cervantes[17]; the down-to-earth Juan Soldado is a distant relative of Sancho Panza. Bearing in mind how successfully he translated

Bernal Díaz, we may wonder how talented a story-teller was lost because Heredia did not persevere more energetically and resolutely with this kind of writing, even if it had been only translation. As regards composing original stories, perhaps it is true that he did not have enough inventiveness. He was the gifted amateur in the full sense of that term. With *Juan Soldado* he showed again his fundamental self-effacement: he was content to achieve an excellent translation and let it speak for itself.

IV

HEREDIA'S REPUTATION AND INFLUENCE

The last chapter of this book offers a brief selection of opinions about our poet with the aim of indicating main trends in Heredia criticism over a period of some fifty years. To examine and assess these opinions is to be acutely reminded of certain truisms: that particular views commonly reveal almost as much about their holders as about the work or person surveyed, that admiration and distaste are often partisan or partial, that objectivity in literary criticism is an almost impossible and perhaps an undesirable or naïve notion. Where would poetry be without involvement of feeling and taste to a point that can seem to preclude real grasp of others' criteria? The worst fate for a poet is doubtless indifference, which may take various forms, one of which is to be elevated to the ranks of the minor immortals in the pantheon of poets and then to remain there only quickly visited or respectfully acknowledged as society, poetry and taste undergo profound changes. This has been Heredia's lot, after a period from 1893 until about 1920 or 1925 when he not only enjoyed great renown but was widely read and appreciated.

He was clearly liked or loved by nearly all who knew him. It is surprisingly difficult to find adverse comment on his character, even when one allows for the fact that many of those who wrote about him from personal knowledge were friends. It has been noted that the sonnets were quite well known some time before the appearance of *Les Trophées* in 1893 both through publication in periodicals and through Heredia's animated recitations. Comment on him before 1893 was often from Parnassians who naturally looked on a fellow-poet with some indulgence. Thus Mendès's amusingly enthusiastic description of 1884 underlines several features in the sonnets: their bright colours, strong sonority and jewel-like perfection of form, in short, some of their Parnassian characteristics. Mendès is the forerunner of many who will reaffirm his points with enthusiasm or disdain, according to taste, and with equal disregard for other aspects of Heredia's art. In 1886, Jules Lemaître is less whole-heartedly metaphoric than

Mendès and more simply exact as he sets Heredia in a general perspective of epic glorification of the past, stresses the magnificence of the evocations but pinpoints the inherently exciting tension between epic theme and classically taut form. In 1889 Charles Morice's much quoted sentence reaffirmed observations made by Mendès and Lemaître from a viewpoint that was to be most remembered and much used by those wanting to criticize *Les Trophées* for their lack of 'thought' and their excessive theatricality.

Other Parnassians or sympathizers with *Le Parnasse* are represented by the novelists Paul Bourget and Anatole France. Though he was the author of the novel *Le Disciple* (1889), a supposed indictment of Taine's positivist philosophy, Bourget is positivist enough as he emphasizes the union in Heredia of *poésie* and *science*, a combination to which attention will be repeatedly drawn by later critics speaking of Heredia's time at the *Ecole des Chartes* and the wealth of knowledge needed to provide the material on which his art was so often based. Anatole France knew his Parnassian poets well, having, like Bourget, been one himself: he brings out Heredia's plastic sense of outline and colour, pushing this observation just short of the point which will later be transformed by others into a criticism of Heredia's alleged impassivity. Verlaine's views in 1892 are well worth our attention, partly because he had begun himself as a keen Parnassian in the 1860s and could therefore write with understanding of Heredia but mostly because he was a great poet, perceptive and generous enough to recognize a good poet when he saw one, even if his style was very different from the one Verlaine himself had by then reached. He notes Heredia's attachment to the heroic values of distant, more chivalrous ages but sets him firmly in the more recent context of Leconte de Lisle's precise, compact art with its emphasis on *le vers bien fait*. The decorous grandiloquence of many sonnets in *Les Trophées* is well observed by a poet whose genius did not usually lie in that direction. Verlaine also makes an important point to be echoed by the Symbolist poet Gustave Kahn in 1905, that the young Symbolist poets of the 1890s approved of *Les Trophées* 'en dépit de sa versification tout à fait romantique et classique qui doit leur paraître un peu surannée' and, he adds, with eclectic wisdom, 'ce dont je les blâmerais,

car toute forme est bonne du moment qu'elle est belle'.[1] By the
time *Les Trophées* appeared in 1893, of course, the Parnassians
were no longer the centre of attention in poetry and the impetus
even of the new movement, Symbolism, had largely spent itself.

The high point for the reputation of *Les Trophées* was undoubtedly reached during the time immediately following their
appearance. 5000 copies of the first edition were sold in the first
few hours; in the following months, 172 articles were published
on the collection.[2] England contributed one of the earliest and
most favourable in April 1894, from Edmund Gosse in *The
Contemporary Review*. He congratulated the Académie française
on electing Heredia in preference to Zola:

> The election of M. de Heredia to the French Academy is an important
> and critical event in the imaginative history of our time, because it is a
> public statement of the value set by a group of men of high and yet
> dissimilar intellectual character on work that is superlatively well done,
> on the work of a craftsman who has not allowed himself to be hurried or
> disturbed by any pressure from without, who has not cared to move an
> inch from his path to please the many or the few, who has spent half
> a lifetime in the pursuit of a splendid perfection, a faultless magnificence
> in concentrated and chiselled verse. It is the occasional appearance, in
> our slipshod world, of artists so consummate as M. de Heredia that keeps
> poetry from being degraded to a mere shabby volubility (p.472).

The body of the article is no less laudatory as Gosse gives a
competent general introduction to *Les Trophées*, praising their
'magnificent precision', distinguishing the 'objective', 'external
or decorative' sonnets of Heredia from the 'introspective or
philosophical' ones of poets like Sully Prudhomme and joining
so many other critics in seeing *Les Trophées* as a fine 'gallery of
paintings'. In other comments too, Gosse cogently captures some
of the main points and attitudes that will characterize French
criticism of the collection:

> For him the symbol must be clear, brilliant, physical; he has no
> pleasure in mysticism or in the twilight of the intelligence. And this,
> indeed, must be confessed at once, that those who seek for tender notes
> and sunken lights, the vague sympathies of the soul, the melancholy
> music of experience, may go elsewhere; the poet of *Les Trophées* is not
> for them. No man has less been touched by the malady of the age, no one

is less attracted to the unknown and the distressful. M. de Heredia gazes straight at clear and beautiful things seen in a blaze of light; almost every sonnet of his gives an impression of translucent air and brilliant sunshine. Alone, among French poets of today, the prevailing note of his work is joyous and heroic (p. 477).

Each of the sections of Heredia's collection is briefly evoked with elegant enthusiasm. The only objection Gosse thinks might be brought against Heredia the poet is the result of his very perfection, 'this uniform strenuousness. One wishes that all were not quite so metallic in sound, so sumptuous in colour, so radiantly and sonorously objective' (p. 482). In fact, all the sonnets are not so, but we shall see this particular reservation recur quite frequently in France. It will gather force and join others as the century ends—witness, in 1899, the words from Arthur Symons (see p. 128) which are a sort of funeral oration to Parnassian poetry in general and to Heredia's sonnets in particular as the influence of Symbolism spreads through Europe.

Gustave Kahn recalls that the reception accorded to *Les Trophées* in France was either enthusiastic or at least respectfully appreciative of the sonnets' merits. The early total praise adumbrates what will become the commonplaces of Heredia criticism. For A. Albalat (see p. 127), Heredia is not just a painter but a sculptor: these Parnassian metaphors express our poet's neglect of thought or speculation, his essentially artistic preoccupations both in subject and manner, his concern for colour, shape and outline. Henry Bordeaux's contribution in 1895 is a quite sensitive, judicious, if rather prolix, attempt to depict Heredia's virtues as a poet and set them in some literary perspective. Bordeaux gives due importance to the aesthetic pleasure which *Les Trophées* so markedly embody, not just through images but through sounds and implicit attitudes; he is on firm ground when he highlights the powerful contrasts in the sonnets, but these merits in Heredia are given their proper place at the expense of some exaggeration, to the point where Bordeaux affirms that Heredia does not like shade or darkness and knows nothing of perspective. This enthusiasm, shown by Mendès earlier as well as by Edmund Gosse, for Heredia's undoubted love of bright colours and lights, as well as of sonorous effects in some of his sonnets, leads many critics to underestimate other sonnets—in 'Epigrammes et Bucoliques' ('La Grèce et la Sicile') or 'Sonnets épigraphiques' ('Rome et les Barbares')—which illustrate different qualities and particularly gentleness and restrained half-tones.

But as early as 1894 the occasional critical voice made itself heard. Ludovic Hamilo is the first of several to dismiss what he admits are the marvellous pictures and music in the sonnets in order to condemn Heredia's lack of involvement in topical issues and in 'life' as it is experienced by most people: the readers' souls are untouched and the poetry will not survive. Hamilo's views are the obverse of those praising Heredia for his rare capacity to bring vivid life to some objects that were before seen as recondite (cf. Gaston Deschamps, p. 128); it is Hamilo's criteria that make the difference. It was not until the following year that the first really strong criticism appeared, from Raoul Rosières. His article in *La Revue bleue* was one of the best that had yet appeared, informed, intelligent, sensitive and interestingly hostile. The analysis of Heredia's indebtedness to Leconte de Lisle and the evolution he accomplished towards dramatic concision is well founded, but the summary judgements of taste are very contestable. Heredia is criticized for not having 'la fantaisie interminable' of Hugo or Leconte de Lisle's particular capacity to penetrate the souls of past civilizations. What irritates Rosières is Heredia's verbal control. Against this are set the 'imprévu' of Hugo and the 'images inattendues' of Leconte de Lisle; Heredia's precision is exaggerated to give a picture of implacable rigidity. The references by Rosières, towards the end of his article, to the ideal poet as 'une sorte de voyant révélant aux hommes un monde inconnu ou clamant à voix divine ce qu'ils sentent ou ce qu'ils pensent' shows how the perspectives have begun to change since the 1860s and 1870s: the seer Hugo, the *voyant* Rimbaud, the delicately subjective and—it was thought—spontaneous Verlaine provide, for a certain number of readers, the new criteria by which Heredia is a verbal artisan, a mere stylist, with no 'soul', no message to communicate, a poet whose values are irremediably tied to the past. Leaving on one side the attachment to the past, we here meet exactly the reaction to Victor Hugo's *Les Orientales* and to some of Gautier's poetry when, in the 1830s and 1840s, it was seen as *poésie visible* or *poésie matérialiste*. Rosières is the voice of the future, already attuning himself to Verlaine's more restlessly personal and Rimbaud's more oneirically 'committed' manners. Later criticism of Heredia will dwell strongly on this reproach of being so consciously in command of what he is doing in a sonnet, so deliberately exploiting his 'habileté de practicien' that he must lack the heart of a 'true poet'. For good measure, Rosières adds his dislike of those sonnets where the sound and rhythmic effects are strongly present. He does incidentally admit that if poetic virtuosity is acknowledged along with vigorous clarity of colour and outline, then Heredia has written some of the finest sonnets in French. Could he have read with care and really thought about 'La Prière du mort' and 'L'Esclave' ('La Grèce et la Sicile'), 'Hortorum Deus III' ('Rome et les Barbares') or 'Floridum mare' ('La Nature et le rêve')?

At first sight, Georges Pellissier, in 1898, is more generously favourable in his judgement than Rosières, but his viewpoint is not so different. Heredia is praised for some of the points that have already been well noted by others and will be tirelessly repeated in histories of literature. He is at one and the same time poet, painter and sculptor. He has virtuosity: the word is taking on a more pejorative overtone as it is repeated to describe Heredia's excessive skill or control and the pleasure shown by his manipulation of aesthetic effects. For the first time in Heredia criticism, *artiste* is opposed to *poète*, Heredia being seen more as the former than the latter. He is the worse for allegedly having no trace of *tendresse*, *sympathie du cœur* or *inquiétude de l'esprit*. I would argue that elements of all three are discreetly present in *Les Trophées*, especially the first two, but Pellissier is fonder of sharp outlines than Heredia himself. The formulation 'Malherbe flamboyant'—to capture Heredia's supposed combination of syntactic correctness and epic splendour—is tersely witty but Pellissier's notions are absurd when he argues that the Parnassians saw poetry as just stricter prose or when he regrets the absence in Heredia of 'négligences divines', which amounts to claiming that excellence or even perfection is reprehensible. What is needed is a clearer definition of the kind of perfection Heredia wanted to achieve. Verlaine, Rimbaud and Heredia are all three fine poets in their different ways: one of a good critic's roles is to show their differences so that the readers who like all three can share and understand the pleasure afforded by each of them. The short extract from Lanson repeats Pellissier's conclusions and we reflect that for generations of students until the Second World War Lanson's history of French literature was a kind of bible.

By the early years of this century, Heredia was already coming to be regarded as a classic. A seal of some sort was clearly set on his reputation by Max Jasinski's important *Histoire du sonnet en France* (1903). Not only was the study dedicated to the master sonneteer Heredia but many of his sonnets were highly praised and used by Jasinski as excellent illustrations of particular points or effects. Some of Jasinski's ideas concerning imitative harmony are questionable but his examination of Heredia's art is quite balanced and thorough, even if his main considerations are by 1903 no longer so original. He stresses above all Heredia's consummate artistry, his blending of erudition and the sensuous power of words. Yet even Jasinski describes the sonnets as 'dédaigneux d'éloquence, exempts d'émotion', but the description is no longer a charge levelled against the poet. Only two years later, Kahn more soundly wrote of Heredia's 'beaux dons d'éloquence continue' and later in our century Heredia seemed very eloquent, too eloquent, to readers whose tastes had been transformed by Symbolism and Surrealism. Jasinski does at least reach the strictly accurate conclusion: 'c'est peut-être la perfection de la pure poésie parnassienne'. More cogently accurate still is Emile Faguet's assessment within a week of Heredia's death. Calmly affirming that Heredia is 'un très grand poète', he mostly avoids vague and inflated terms of praise or blame to give a brief analysis of two principal aspects of Heredia's poetry, its place in a classical tradition going back through Chénier and Ronsard to Greek and Roman literature and then its originality and modernity in 'son art du ramassé', which clearly covers not just pictorial and sculptural qualities, but what I have called Heredia's dramatic immediacy, with all its ramifications. And Faguet's conclusion is balanced and fair: Heredia's place is not among the giants of French poetry because, by intuitive self-restriction, his poetry is limited in range and scope.

Equally judicious is the article in the same year by Gustave Kahn, the Symbolist poet who was one of the inaugurators of *le vers libre.* Twelve years after the publication of *Les Trophées*, it is becoming easier to see Heredia in the broad context of French poetry. Kahn makes the important point that *Les Trophées*—'ce très beau livre'—stood out in 1893 as triumphantly indifferent to immediately contemporary preoccupations and appeared refreshingly above the fray of current poets eager to chase the latest theory concerning poetic rhythm or to be the voice of the people. Heredia's influence is linked with the classical revival attempted by the poets of the *école romane* at the beginning of the 1890s, Jean Moréas, Ernest Raynaud, Charles Maurras, Raymond de la Tailhède and Maurice du Plessys; in fact, there was no close collaboration between them and Heredia. Kahn explains that a poet like Léon Dierx may have shown qualities comparable with Heredia's but did not approach anything resembling the success of *Les Trophées* because he was still enmeshed in Baudelaire's anguish and Leconte de Lisle's pessimism. With all the influences at work on him, Heredia was supremely himself. He boldly adhered to his classical inspiration. The filiation between Heredia, Leconte de Lisle, Gautier and Chénier is carefully traced, as is the influence of painters like Chassériau and Gustave Moreau— 'cet art niellé et idéologique tout ensemble, ornemental et décoratif, épris de vision précise et lointaine'. Kahn recapitulates the recent history of the sonnet form in France and draws sensitive distinctions between its use by Baudelaire, Banville and Heredia. For Baudelaire, 'le sonnet est, le plus souvent, la mise en œuvre d'une tonalité musicale du sentiment, le moyen de fixer une nuance', whereas Banville used it for portraits, and then not so frequently, while Heredia brought the form to a peak of dramatic, suggestive conciseness. Mallarmé's conception of the sonnet is recalled, whereby the climax should come in the penultimate line. Heredia took the view that it should be left to the last line: 'à son point de vue de plasticien il avait parfaitement raison, car il déterminait ainsi d'un trait d'énergie, d'un accent violent, le relief du tableau qu'il voulait obtenir'. Kahn argues that Mallarmé and Heredia were both justified because they looked for different qualities in the sonnet form, 'Mallarmé y mettant des idées et des rêveries, et J.-M. de Heredia des évocations de décor et de tableau'. With admirable penetration, Kahn stresses that the mythological figures evoked by Heredia are not mere stylistic exercises or displays of erudition, but, as in the conception of the Centaurs, powerful embodiments of human and animal passion. After summing up Heredia's principal qualities in the extract quoted in Chapter VI, Kahn tackles the allegation made by some that Heredia lacked imagination. Anticipating one of the arguments of Valéry's vigorous defence of Mallarmé against the criticism of having composed too little, Kahn emphasizes that we must try to appreciate Heredia's own point of view:

Si, pour d'autres, le labeur de l'écrivain consiste à produire et à propager le plus d'idées possible, pour lui le devoir était de prouver sa valeur par quelque chose qui lui appartînt tout à fait en propre et qui fût achevé, définitif (pp. 510–11).

Kahn's article is excellent, one of the most informed Heredia has ever received. Baudelaire believed that good poets inevitably have the makings of good critics. If Kahn's own poetry was not of the highest order, his sensitive discrimination enabled him to assess Heredia's strength and limitations and to understand that what is called his classicism was not a tired pursuit of outworn models but a vital, unifying force at work in all he wrote.

Heredia's emerging international stature, already marked by Edmund Gosse's article in 1894, and the already developing tendency to rank him among the significant poets of the past are attested in 1907 by John C. Bailey's sympathetic portrayal in his study of nine French poets for the British public. Bailey has nothing very original to say but his popularization quite eloquently, if a little pompously, captured many of the virtues already noted in *Les Trophées* and particularly the sonnets' magniloquence.

Apart from Gustave Kahn's, Raoul Rosières' article of 1895 had been the most substantially sensitive, if rather wrongheaded, yet devoted to Heredia. Eugène Langevin's study in 1907 was even more thorough, resembling Rosières' both in its penetration and its blend of praise and censure. It is essential to understand Langevin's criteria. He accords the highest praise to Heredia's brilliant translation of Bernal Díaz (cf. Chapter III of the present work) and of '*le Señor soldado*, conte andalou d'une superbe jovialité', but in the field of poetry he sees Heredia as 'un homme de peu d'invention'. It is a pity, he claims, anticipating Bernard Shaw's celebrated advice, that Heredia did not each day make himself write several pages of a novel, quickly and spontaneously, with no corrections, even if he were to have burned the pages later. In this way,

le poète se fût acquis peu à peu le jaillissement des idées et sentiments poétiques, qui, par suite de la pauvreté de son fond et d'habitudes propres à développer les facultés critiques et accessoires, non les créatrices et principales, n'ont jamais été chez lui qu'un petit filet bien maigre. (p. 56).

Such a masterly failure to understand Heredia's fundamental attitudes does not at first sight augur well for Langevin's appreciation of *Les Trophées*. The point made by Rosières is taken up again more strongly, that Heredia sought to be too conscious and controlled in his composition, so that he cannot recapture the sublime naïveté necessary to do justice to the epic subject of a poem like 'Les Conquérants de l'or'. 'Comme on sent bien qu'il n'y croit pas! Un monsieur très docte s'est appliqué.' With this standpoint regarding this particular poem, I have some sympathy. Langevin gives a comprehensive historical analysis of Heredia's debt to the past: to the themes or prosody of Vigny, Hugo, Leconte de Lisle, Banville and Chénier, the very tone of elegant sadness in Racine and the Greek poets, the debt to lesser figures like Louis Bouilhet and Sully Prudhomme. These observations are extremely well founded but the theoretical perspective put on them is almost exclusively condemnatory: Heredia's absorption of influences is made far too deliberate and conscious and when it is conceded that Heredia equalled and surpassed predecessors like Leconte de Lisle and Banville, he is censured for having done so and inaccurately blamed for having done nothing else. 'Achever ce qui dans les poètes antérieurs semblait le plus achevé; surpasser ses prédécesseurs là où ils paraissaient s'être surpassés eux-mêmes, telle est la devise arborée de Heredia imitateur et il n'est guère que cela.' What Faguet called the 'art du ramassé' is well illustrated by Langevin, particularly with regard to Heredia's superiority over Banville and especially well in the matter of prosody; Heredia achieves maximum density of effect through simultaneous attention to ideas, rhythms and sounds. Langevin's natural sensitivity allows him to grasp what is excellent in Heredia much more successfully than his initial theoretical premises might have led us to believe possible. He thus proceeds to ask: 'Peut-on dire qu'il ait, le premier, fait donner au dernier vers l'impression d'un élargissement brusque et comme infini?' His taste is delicate enough to record the 'très caressantes et très fluides mélodies virgiliennes ou raciniennes' in *Les Trophées* but he does not like the intensity of some sound effects—'les mots suent dans ses sonnets'—because it conveys for him too strong an impression of self-conscious artificiality. As by Rosières earlier, Verlaine is seen in the background as the ideal modern poet, gentle, sincere, musical, wistful, the 'natural' poet.[3] While noting the skill with which the climaxes of Heredia's sonnets are organized, Langevin objects to the frequency and hence predictability of the procedure. This is certainly a reasonable criticism. Being fond of musical analogies, Langevin might have likened the predictable structure of some sonnets to Rossini's orchestration, as we can sense from early on all the preparations that will lead to the appearance, like a jack-in-the-box (to use Langevin's image), of the grand, definitive climax. Langevin characterizes extemely well Heredia's process of stylization leading to a type of heraldic beauty: the attribution of 'synthèses merveilleuses' is cogent and purely approbatory. The conclusion of this important article sounded a warning note which we can now appreciate had great force: the aristocratic *tenue* of *Les Trophées*, their values derived from a doubtless admirable aestheticism and a strongly classical culture entailed a dangerous distance from more direct and vigorous sources of life and feeling. We know now that the dangers were to materialize in the revaluations in poetry which the twentieth century was to bring, with its emphasis on irrationality, spontaneity and sometimes more popular inspirations.

Léautaud, the quotations from whose diary are dated 1908 and 1938, exemplifies the impatience of many readers, *littérateurs* and general public, with esoteric interests in art and the traditional values of past ages. The poet should be 'un homme de son époque', he should 'parler des choses de son époque'. How the Parnassians of the 1860s and 1870s had disdained such a viewpoint! For Mallarmé's luminously profound affirmation

that poems are made not from ideas but from words the simplistic Léautaud has no time and perhaps no proper understanding. For him, Heredia and Valéry are pompous word-spinners. We are at least now sure that for many discriminating readers Mallarmé and Valéry are poets of the greatest stature and that Heredia has a place not too far behind them, however less significant and subtle his genius may be.

The first decade of this century therefore saw some of Heredia's main qualities as a poet understood, examined and, for the most part, praised. The years 1910 and 1911 marked a period of deeper study, erudite and academic in the main, combining specialist knowledge of history and literature and some very relevant consideration of artistic features in the sonnets. Four names stand out, the Swede Emil Zilliacus: 'José-Maria de Heredia et *l'Anthologie grecque*'; Raoul Thauziès: 'Etude sur les sources de J.-M. de Heredia dans les cinquante-sept premiers sonnets des *Trophées*'; Joseph Vianey: 'Les Sonnets grecs de Heredia' and René Pichon: 'L'Antiquité romaine et la poésie française à l'époque parnassienne' (cf. Bibliography). Zilliacus threw quite new light on the influences at work from antiquity. Before his study, the influences had been seen as almost exclusively those of Greek or Roman art, such as statues, vases or bas-reliefs. He showed convincingly that the influence was just as much literary as artistic, resulting particularly from Heredia's reading of the poets of the Greek Anthology, both in the original and in the French translation of Fr. Jacobs (Hachette, 1863).[4] When all allowance has been made for this literary influence, it is important to note that, against Langevin's general charge that Heredia was guilty of almost straight copying of many sources, Zilliacus affirms that the poet rarely transcribed what he found in the epigrams of the Greek Anthology but borrowed from them freely and adapted what he borrowed to his own manner:

La matière souvent aride et maigre des petits poètes de l'hellénisme finissant a été, plus d'une fois, animée et fécondée par l'imagination de Heredia; il y a presque toujours, dans les sonnets du poète français, une poésie plus riche et plus profonde que dans les épigrammes grecques qui lui ont servi de modèles (p. 9).

Thauziès confirms these findings, reaffirming that Heredia's

sources are varied and often combined in one particular sonnet. Vianey's analysis of the primitive meaning of the myths treated by Heredia in figures like Perseus and Hercules is very interesting and convincing enough, though he perhaps tends to exaggerate the significance of the early meaning for our understanding and enjoyment of the sonnets.[5] Vianey's comments are very sound on the sonnets' dramatic aspects. Heredia knew how to avoid 'tableaux inertes. Les siens se composent devant nous. Il ne décrit donc pas, il raconte':

> Puisque toujours chez lui, il y a une véritable action, prise, naturellement, très près du dénouement; il y a une péripétie, qui change tout, donne à tout une face imprévue; la dernière phrase apporte, en même temps qu'un tableau saisissant, une explication nécessaire (p. 769).

Chénier's influence, along with that of Victor Hugo, is noted as being stronger than Leconte de Lisle's in Heredia's characteristic fusion of action, curiosity and interest and in the suddenness of many of the sonnets' beginnings and the suspense created. But Heredia's poems have more colour than Chénier's, more technical *mots justes*; in general, Heredia's art, uniting so well harmony of sound and ideas, is much more complex than Leconte de Lisle's or Chénier's. Pichon's study complements the work of the three critics just discussed, with particular reference to Latin literature and Heredia's rare capacity to bring together 'd'un côté, la précision technique des détails matériels, d'autre part, l'intelligence de ce qui est essentiel et fondamental'. These four studies from well-informed and sensitive critics do justice to the subtlety of Heredia's art, not simply in what it owes for its inspiration to antiquity but in its original and specifically modern resonances.

On the eve of the First World War, Remy de Gourmont may serve as spokesman for those who are increasingly thinking like Rosières nearly twenty years before and, like Rosières, using Verlaine as an example of a composer of poetry that is personal, musical, spontaneous and thereby refreshingly different from Heredia's lofty sonnets with their allegedly overbearing splendour and coldly impersonal perfection. But Heredia's following is still great and includes those who, like his son-in-law Henri de Régnier, himself a Symbolist poet of some significance, can appreciate the

quieter and more tender tones in *Les Trophées* and help to correct
the earlier excessive insistence on Heredia's sonorous heroism.
It is particularly during the second decade of this century that
those who knew Heredia well begin to publish their recollections,
like Léon Barracand in 1914 and Antoine Albalat in 1919.[6]
Though these evocations cannot match some of the studies already
discussed in the examination of Heredia's poetic talent, their
combination of personal experience, anecdote and gossip is
extremely useful for our understanding of Heredia the man, his
views on art and his relations with others, both social and more
specifically literary. It is, for example, amusing and instructive
to learn that Heredia was a little jealous that one of Barracand's
sonnets, dedicated to Leconte de Lisle, had pleased the Master;
he showed relief when Barracand explained he did not intend
to write any more. Heredia's astonishment and pale countenance
are amusingly significant when he learns just after the publication of *Les Trophées* that 'Les Conquérants de l'or' contains
four lines with four masculine rhymes that are consecutive, not
following the *alternance des rimes*. The fault was hastily corrected.

At the end of the second decade of the twentieth century
worthwhile studies of Heredia that are specifically literary were
still appearing, such as Fernand Brodel's 'L'Elégie chez Heredia',
where the definition of elegiac is perhaps too narrow but where the
analyses of particular sonnets are very sensitive. According to
Brodel, the brevity and conciseness demanded by the sonnet form
are not easy to reconcile with sadness and regret which tend in
any case to disappear beneath the strong colours and sound
effects in many of Heredia's sonnets. Brodel is thus prolonging
a criticism made years earlier by Bordeaux and Rosières: 'la
beauté des images et la fanfare des syllabes font tort à la sincérité
de l'émotion'. To talk of emotional sincerity in this way is to
misunderstand the deliberate nature of Heredia's exploitation of
language for the reader's delectation. If the criterion of sincerity
is to be introduced, it needs to be clearly defined so that the
differences between the standpoints of Brodel and Heredia can be
appreciated. For Brodel the result is that only a dozen or so
sonnets are regarded as being truly elegiac, the epigrammatic
sonnets in 'La Grèce et la Sicile' and a few others like 'Marsyas',
'L'Exilée' and 'Epitaphe':

Ces sonnets du 'mode mineur' se recommandent par un rythme plus souple, la douceur caressante des syllabes, la terminaison plaintive de la rime qui s'unissent pour 'correspondre' à l'émotion du poète et former chacun, sous la diversité changeante des vers, un ensemble d'une parfaite harmonie mélancolique (p. 120).

The reminiscences of Baudelaire (*correspondre*) and Verlaine (*mode mineur*)[7] show the further movement made by 1920 away from Parnassian criteria towards an implicit acceptance of ideas and ideals embodied in Symbolist poetry. Yet the model Brodel has in mind is mostly classical in nature, simple and free of *ornements* in order to allow us to 'mieux discerner le dessin du rythme, du chant intérieur, comme dans une nature dépouillée par l'hiver on aperçoit mieux les lignes essentielles du paysage'.

The most thorough contribution yet made to Heredia studies has been the thesis in three volumes by Miodrag Ibrovac, in 1923 (see Bibliography). Fifty years later, we can see more clearly how influenced Ibrovac was by nineteenth-century critical methods, those for instance of Taine and Lanson: his whole systematic approach and rather deterministic judgements now seem to give off a faint odour of positivism, so that Nerval is seen as a 'poète de second ordre' (ii, p. 484) and Heredia's 'philosophy' is earnestly analysed (ii, pp. 386–403). His three volumes brought to light much new material—above all, letters and poems—which is interpreted with intelligence and method to provide the most comprehensive study of Heredia in existence. For those wishing to study him in any detail, it is an indispensable source both of basic information about his life, publications and critical works about him and of mature reflection and judgement whose main shortcoming is not only that more recent critical standpoints could inevitably not be taken into account but that it did not, even in 1923, reflect full awareness of the transformation Baudelaire, Verlaine, Rimbaud and Mallarmé had begun.[8] Ibrovac can scarcely be criticized for this limitation: Surrealism was literally happening as his volumes were published.

1925 brought the inauguration of a bust of Heredia in the Luxembourg gardens in Paris; it was the occasion for a sympathetic flurry of articles in newspapers and periodicals such as *Le Temps*, *Le Journal des débats*, the literary supplement of *Le Gaulois du dimanche*, *Le Figaro* and the literary supplement of *Le*

Figaro and *Le Journal*.[9] Nothing original or important emerges from these short-lived writings, which are all understandably laudatory and take up some of the points, biographical and literary, that we have already examined. 1925 was thus a celebration of Heredia the classic sonneteer. But amid the pious recapitulations there are incidental comments which throw interesting light on the evolution of Heredia's reputation and of the thinking of the older generation who loved the kind of poetry he stood for. In *Le Temps* of 19 October 1925 a certain P.S. (doubtless Paul Souday), after describing the unveiling of the bust in the Luxembourg gardens and praising Heredia's brevity and objectivity as a poet, gives his opinion that *Les Trophées* provide a good lesson for the wildly subjective poets of 1925 and those writers of novels and plays who have no 'point d'appui ni de contrôle'. The literary supplement of *Le Figaro*, on 31 October, printed three unpublished sonnets—'Ménalque', 'Damète' and 'Palémon'—allegedly by Heredia and thought to have been composed between 1870 and 1893. It is reported that the original manuscript of these sonnets was lost during the war. If they are Heredia's, they are curiously uninspired and give no particular sense of his presence. The sonnets are accorded more praise than they are worth and—significantly, for our understanding of the development of Heredia criticism—it is argued that they prove how wrong are those who see Heredia as 'cet orfèvre au cœur sec, ce froid burineur de vers "impeccables mais sans âmes" [sic] que peignent aux jeunes gens tant de manuels d'histoire littéraire'. I sympathize with the assertion that 'nous avons bien peur que ceux qui appellent Heredia un poète éclatant mais froid, ne connaissent de lui que deux ou trois sonnets'.

The mention of *manuels d'histoire littéraire* is appropriate at this point. Articles still appeared on Heredia in the 1930s and beyond. Guignard and Labarthe (see p. 133) are among those who celebrated in 1943 the centenary of Heredia's birth and the fiftieth year of the publication of *Les Trophées*. What they had to say is not new but it is quite well said; they were writing about a poet who seemed to have been dead for more than thirty-eight years. Wherever the exercise of *explication de texte* is practised, that is, not just in classrooms and lecture-rooms but in periodicals, particularly for teachers, we encounter what in this country we often call commentaries devoted to Heredia sonnets. In 1907, we have seen, Langevin ended his article on a warning note regarding the attitude that would be taken towards *Les Trophées* by future generations. His warning included the following slightly sardonic estimate:

Son art raffiné et qui se prête très bien à l'analyse, qui même la provoque, fera que ses sonnets resteront, un temps que l'on ne peut évaluer, comme curiosités, et aussi comme pièces de démonstrations entre les mains des professeurs dans des éditions savantes où variantes et indications de sources tiendront les trois quarts de la place. Ils auront aussi une grande valeur documentaire, extrêmement récapulatifs qu'ils sont de toutes les acquisitions qu'ont faites les diverses techniques du sonnet et de l'alexandrin de Ronsard à Leconte de Lisle, et de notre érudition historique contemporaine, et de notre sentiment de l'art ancien et moderne.

The First World War blew up millions of men and began the process of blowing away a whole culture. Futurism, just before the war, Dadaism, during and just after the war, and, in the 1920s, Surrealism were some of the easily identified groupings of artists who were to challenge some of the assumptions of previous ages: rationality, order, tradition. At one level, the challenge was political, against the settled capitalist or bourgeois system that was thought to have oppressed millions of ordinary people for generations and through its muddled selfishness and concentration on material profit to have nearly led to the destruction of Western European society. At another level, the challenge was metaphysical, developing and deepening tendencies set in train by art before the First World War and by the findings of thinkers like Freud whose interpretation of human motivation was to persuade many that we are driven by hidden, unconscious forces more than by any resolve of the will. Poets like Rimbaud and Lautréamont were to be given pride of place by the Surrealists partly because they had anticipated long before the end of the nineteenth century the Surrealists' own addiction to delirious, hallucinatory irrationality. The considerations that were to replace those of the past are now commonplace in our own contemporary histories of literature and culture. The movement called Surrealism was to have lasting effects and most importantly perhaps on those poets who did not remain pure Surrealists but returned to 'literature' deeply affected by the movement to which they had belonged in the 1920s and 1930s. A complicating factor is the time lag involved in the diffusion and assessment of new tendencies: for most of the reading public in the years before and even after the Second World War, much of what was good in French poetry was still represented by a line of poets from Ronsard to Baudelaire, Verlaine and perhaps Heredia. For some today, this is still the case. But for many of the new poets who were writing in the 1920s and later, the assumptions of Heredia's day were gone for ever. For novelists like Malraux, for poets like Eluard, however different their preoccupations and talents, a new world had begun, frightening and exhilarating by turns in the challenge it presented of total freedom to destroy and to recreate. For many poets, ontological anguish and rapture swept away what to them now appeared as the petty, hopelessly rationalist, naïvely ordered poetry their predecessors had inherited from an age which had little resemblance to the society in travail that was to lead to the Second World War and, after it, to an acceleration of the speed with which we were separating ourselves from the hierarchies that had characterized both literature and society when Heredia was alive. Some three hundred years separated Ronsard and Heredia; seventy years separate us now from Heredia. In many ways, he was nearer in spirit to the French Renaissance poets than our age is to him.

Small wonder that Heredia has quickly passed into history as a classic. In 1936, in his *Histoire de la littérature française de 1789 à nos jours*, Albert Thibaudet wrote of Heredia's technical perfection in the sonnet form 'dont [il] est devenu le patron, à un tel point qu'après lui le sonnet est entré dans le sommeil, qu'il dort encore' (p. 330). Heredia is found in countless anthologies of French poetry between the wars, represented by a number of sonnets that tends to decrease as the anthologies approach the present. Thus Pierre de Boisdeffre's *Une Anthologie vivante de la littérature d'aujourd'hui: la poésie française de Baudelaire à nos jours* (Perrin, 1966) has poems by Hugo, Nerval, Lautréamont, Rimbaud, Mallarmé, Verlaine, Samain, Corbière, Laforgue, Claudel, Valéry and many others up to Aimé Césaire and Yves Bonnefoy. It has no Heredia and no Leconte de Lisle.[10] In the implicit opinion of Boisdeffre, concerned with the continuing evolution of French poetry and therefore with what he sees as its source of vitality for the future, it is as though *Le Parnasse* never existed. Yet the most cogently simple conclusion concerning *Les Trophées* is perhaps the one reached by Jasinski: 'c'est peut-être la perfection de la pure poésie parnassienne'.

Literary influences are notoriously difficult to detect with precision and many critics would question the worth even of the attempt. It is not easy to separate the general influence of *Le Parnasse* and the many poets associated with it from the ascendancy of any one member; this is particularly true if we have in mind something as comprehensive as themes and aspirations. If we narrow down our focus to the actual form of the sonnet, we observe its great popularity during the last quarter of the nineteenth century and the prevalence of collections of sonnets. But where does the influence of a given sonneteer, say Banville, end and Heredia's begin? Any sonnet on a historical theme or evoking an *objet d'art*, revealing a heroic, sonorous, pictorially sumptuous or dramatically decorative quality—and there were very many of these—is a candidate for the label of Heredia influence. Such labelling, for what it is worth, is doubtless right and is perhaps the strongest evidence of Heredia's influence. We have seen that the final decade of the last century and the first two of this marked the apogee of both readers' and critics' interest in Heredia and that there was then some falling away. Ibrovac's monumental study appeared appropriately in 1923, towards the end of this period. He too modestly affirms that his examination of Heredia's influence (ii, pp. 501–48) gives no more than summary suggestions. It is true that he could not possibly foresee all the ramifications of this influence in other countries, nor, for instance, was he able to appreciate the stamp of Heredia in the 1890s on the early poetry and attitudes of as great a poet as Paul Valéry, who was only just emerging as great while Ibrovac was writing. The fact remains that for the period when Heredia's example was most followed Ibrovac accomplished a conscientious task of detection that can best be consulted at source; only a long analysis far exceeding the bounds of this monograph could hope to improve on his and my few main selective points will inevitably follow the many made by him.

The influence of the Parnassians and their sympathizers on each other and their interaction with Heredia as one of them would furnish almost endless matter for speculation. Reminiscences of Heredia sonnets occur in both the poetry and prose of writers like the young Anatole France or Albert Mérat. The painters Claudius Popelin, Emmanuel Lansyer and Jules Breton drew direct, personal inspiration for their sonnets from Heredia, to whom many collections were dedicated, like Henri Rouger's *La Retraite fleurie* (1906) in which the poem 'Les Etapes' lamented the master's death. Heredia's friend Philippe Dufour (Paterne Berrichon) published cycles of sonnets celebrating the ancient towns of France, her dramatic poets and her masterpieces in painting and sculpture (cf. *De Songe en songe*, 1904). A sample list of a dozen books of sonnets published at the turn of the century may be found in Ibrovac's study (ii, p. 503). The imitation of *Les Trophées* is obvious in the titles of the sections of such books, as in *Les Sonnets d'Yalbel, la légende de l'histoire*, by J. Leblay (1904): 'Le Vieil Orient', 'Sparte et Athènes', 'Rome', 'La Gaule'. Particular sonnets in *Les Trophées* gave rise to many imitations. Thus L.-K. Amiel's *Sonnets* (1907) include a 'Bacchante' which picks up images, expressions and rhymes from Heredia's 'Ariane' and 'Bacchanale':

> Au frémissant appel des cymbales d'airain,
> Quand sur le Cithéron la bacchanale antique
> Bondissait, brandissant le thyrse asiatique,
> Roulant comme un torrent vers l'horizon marin,
>
> Le front ensanglanté de la pourpre du vin,
> La ménade entonnait son ode prophétique
> Et nue, échevelée, entraînait, frénétique,
> Les hôtes des forêts dans son rythme divin.
>
> Et fauves et sylvains, ainsi qu'une rafale,
> Lancés, précipitaient leur course triomphale
> Sur les pas enfiévrés des filles de Kadmos.
>
> Et l'air vibrait encor, quand soudain, haletante,
> La gorge en feu, les reins épuisés, la Bacchante
> S'écroulait, enivrée au souffle d'Iacchos.

As regards 'Rome et les Barbares', not only is there a general influence on collections like *Poèmes romains* (see Ibrovac, ii, p. 518)

which their author Frédéric Plessis dedicated to Heredia, but
the very particular inspiration of 'Hortorum Deus' contributes
powerfully, in ideas and vocabulary, to the sonnet 'Le Maraudeur'
in Paul Dandicolle's *Sonnets antiques et modernes* (1905). 'Soir de
bataille' excited many emulators. Ibrovac traces the memory of
Heredia's triptych on Cleopatra in Albert Samain, Paul Dandicolle, Auguste Angellier and Ephraïm Mikhaël. The theme of
'Médaille antique' ('La Nature et le rêve') was also very popular
with other sonneteers, as is shown by the following sestet from
a sonnet by Léonce Depont (*Anthologie Walch*, iii, p. 367):

> Tout passera, la pierre et le marbre et les races
> Et les Dieux, engloutis par les siècles voraces;
> Tout, esclave et tyran, suzerain et vassal,
>
> Mais, au fond de la nuit tragiquement grondante,
> L'Homme entier restera, sublime et colossal,
> Dans un vers de Virgile ou dans un vers de Dante.

To multiply such instances of imitation or influence among
poets seen as attached in some way to Parnassian values would
serve little purpose. None of these poets had Heredia's artistic
genius; few if any of them are now read and few are of lasting
worth in their own right. The important fact is that between
1893 and 1920 it was difficult to write a sonnet without ex-
periencing the awareness and often the influence of *Les Trophées*.
When we consider Heredia's influence on Symbolist poets we
need to remember that there was no sharp point dividing Symbolism and *Le Parnasse*: poets of the stature of Baudelaire and
Mallarmé can be usefully seen as combining features that belong
to Romanticism, *Parnasse* and Symbolism. However resolute
a Parnassian, Heredia was well received by young Symbolist
poets and he contributed to many periodicals associated with
their movement, *La Revue indépendante*, *La Revue blanche*, *L'Ermitage*,
La Jeune France, *La Revue libre* and *Le Mercure de France*. He knew
Mallarmé from early days, when they collaborated in the first
Parnasse contemporain and met in Leconte de Lisle's salon; he
enjoyed Mallarmé's poetry. He was the only important Parnassian
poet to publish poems in the Belgian periodical *La Wallonie* as
well as in *L'Art libre*, and the flourishing school of Belgian poets
at the end of the century was full of admiration for *Les Trophées*.

Many French Symbolists wrote most favourably of Heredia, such as Alfred Poizat, André Fontainas and the poets Henri de Régnier and Gustave Kahn (see Bibliography). The measure of a poet's influence is perhaps better judged by the quality than by the number of poets affected by him. In the case of Heredia, the number was great but the quality too was considerable in view of his influence on Henri de Régnier, Jean Moréas, Albert Samain and Emile Verhaeren (see Ibrovac, ii, pp. 525–33). The revival of interest in late Greek culture and the refined Alexandrianism of writers like Anatole France (cf. his novel *Thaïs*, 1890) and Albert Samain[11] (cf. his poems in *Aux flancs du vase*, 1898) owed something to Heredia's influence though such writers, like Heredia himself, were affected by their reading of the Greek Anthology and the spread of Greek values by Louis Ménard, especially in his *Rêveries d'un païen mystique*, a collection of prose and poetry published in 1876. The poet and novelist Pierre Louÿs (1870–1925) was part of this Alexandrian revival as witnessed by his *Aphrodite* (1896), an elegantly licentious novel about courtesan life in ancient Alexandria. Louÿs became a disciple of Heredia in the 1890s and his poetry shows some Heredia influence (see Ibrovac, ii, p. 611).

But Louÿs was also a great introducer of his young artistic friends to the idols of the day known to him: it was through Louÿs that the young Paul Valéry (1871–1945) came to attend Heredia's salon in the 1890s. The real, if limited, influence of Heredia on the young Valéry requires a longer examination than can be given here, but a few indications will show how Heredia served as a kind of poetic springboard for one of the greatest of all French poets. Towards the end of 1889, Valéry sent to the *Courrier libre* an article, 'Sur la technique littéraire',[12] which shows him influenced by Baudelaire, Edgar Allan Poe and Mallarmé, enthusiastically formulating his conception of the poet as 'un froid savant, presque un algébriste, au service d'un rêveur affiné'. Heredia's virtuosity raises no problem of 'sincerity' for the young Valéry, whose description of his ideal poetry reflects the mastery and deliberate exploitation of language's resources found in Heredia's sonnets. According to Valéry at this time, the poet

se gardera de jeter sur le papier tout ce que lui soufflera aux minutes heureuses, la Muse Association-des-Idées. Mais, au contraire, tout ce qu'il aura imaginé, senti, songé, échafaudé, passera au crible, sera pesé, épuré, mis à la *forme* et condensé le plus possible pour gagner en force ce qu'il sacrifie en longueur: un sonnet, par exemple, sera une véritable quintessence, un osmazôme, un suc concentré, et cohobé, réduit à quatorze vers, soigneusement *composé* en vue d'un effet final et foudroyant.

Later in his article, Valéry brings in an interesting qualification:

Ainsi, le poème, selon nous, n'a d'autre but que de préparer son dénouement. Nous ne pouvons mieux le comparer qu'aux degrés d'un autel magnifique, aux marches de porphyre que domine le Tabernacle. L'ornement, les cierges, les orfèvreries, les fumées d'encens—tout s'élance, tout est disposé pour fixer l'attention sur l'ostensoir—sur le dernier vers! La composition où cette gradation fait défaut a un aspect fatalement monotone, si riche et savamment ciselée soit-elle. C'est, à notre avis, le grand défaut des sonnets de de [sic] Heredia—par exemple —qui sont *trop beaux*, tout le long, d'un bout à l'autre. Chaque vers a sa vie propre, sa splendeur particulière et détourne l'esprit de l'ensemble.

So much for those critics who think Heredia's sonnets are written only for the effect of the climactic last line! Readers who are acquainted with Valéry's later concern with the art of transitions, the efficacy of the whole passage or poem and with what we may call the dosage of his poetic effects, will not be surprised by this comment. The fact remains that his theory of the sonnet in 1889 is a somewhat liturgically flavoured version of Heredia's practice. And, as Jean Hytier points out,[13] the mature Valéry will modify his theory and implicitly withdraw his reservation of 1889 concerning the too uniform beauty of Heredia's sonnets when he notes in *Autres rhumbs* (1927) that 'le sonnet est fait pour le simultané. Quatorze vers *simultanés*, et fortement désignés comme tels par l'enchaînement et la conservation des rimes: type et structure d'un poème *stationnaire*'.[14] This is what I have tried to indicate by my references to 'dramatic dynamism' and 'dramatic immediacy'. Here, as elsewhere, second thoughts for Valéry were better thoughts.

In a letter to Pierre Louÿs on 2 June 1890 he picks up several of the ideas and expressions in the article he had sent to the *Courrier libre*, affirming that his literary ideal is 'une poésie courte', that

ce sonnet sera un tout complet, soigneusement composé en vue d'un coup de foudre final et décisif. L'adjectif sera toujours le plus évocateur, la sonorité des vers sagement calculée, la pensée souvent enveloppée dans un symbole, voile à peine déchiré par le quatorzième vers [. . .] Tous les moyens seront bons pour produire le maximum d'effet. Bien des procédés oubliés depuis des siècles pourront y être renouvelés (allitérations, répétitions, etc.). D'autres seront empruntés à la musique. . . .[15]

The influence of Heredia is still great but already Valéry is moving further towards a different ideal: in October 1890 he will send two sonnets to Mallarmé.

As regards some of the early poems of Valéry, the influence of Heredia is marked. In a letter to Louÿs of 21 December 1890 he writes of Heredia's greatness and explains:

J'ai envie de faire un sonnet *à Heredia* dont le sujet serait celui-ci: Retour des conquistadors de la vraie Poésie, on entend sur la mer les clairons victorieux, voici les galères dont les voiles se détachent sur le soleil couchant, voici à la proue le vainqueur J. M. de H. dont le nom sonore terminerait glorieusement la pièce rimant avec *irradia* ou *incendia*.[16]

The projected sonnet was written and sent to Heredia on 7 January 1891. It has only recently been published:

Retour des Conquistadors

Le soir victorieux dans les vagues s'allume.
Et, sur l'eau vierge, ainsi que des rires hautains,
Les clairons messagers des fastueux destins
Emerveillent la guivre éparse dans la brume.

Car, de sa voile immense ouvrant la mer qui fume
Le navire se cabre, écrasé du butin,
Sur l'orbe du soleil chimérique et lointain
Et soulève, éperdu, l'éblouissante écume!

Vois! sur la proue en flamme, un grand Conquistador
Vers Palas triomphale élève un lingot d'or
Dont l'éclat se souvient de l'héroïque grève!

Et, gloire de nos yeux, alors irradia
Le pur métal mûri dans les grottes du Rêve,
L'or fabuleux que tu ravis, Heredia! . . .[17]

Another sonnet commonly seen as written under the influence of Heredia is 'César', in *Album de vers anciens* (augmented edition of 1926). It is the only fully regular sonnet in the whole collection:

César, calme César, le pied sur toute chose,
Les poings durs dans la barbe, et l'œil sombre peuplé
D'aigles et des combats du couchant contemplé,
Ton cœur s'enfle, et se sent toute-puissante Cause.

Le lac en vain palpite et lèche son lit rose;
En vain d'or précieux brille le jeune blé;
Tu durcis dans les nœuds de ton corps rassemblé
L'ordre, qui doit enfin fendre ta bouche close.

L'ample monde, au delà de l'immense horizon,
L'Empire attend l'éclair, le décret, le tison
Qui changeront le soir en furieuse aurore.

Heureux là-bas sur l'onde, et bercé du hasard,
Un pêcheur indolent qui flotte et chante, ignore
Quelle foudre s'amasse au centre de César.

The mettlesome figure of Cæsar, the clear, powerfully dramatic images, the strong contrasts and the unusually forceful last line with its strong alliterations are all reminiscent of Heredia. But this and other sonnets by Valéry reveal other traits and notably the beginning of a tendency to express his personal apprehension of great power contained or withheld through images of potenttially explosive force. It is also significant that most of his sonnets, unlike Heredia's, are irregular. Baudelaire and Mallarmé were also influencing his poetry. In brief, we may say that, having absorbed the Heredia influence, Valéry was soon to leave behind what became for him picturesque externals and, though he was to retain all his life a love of concentrated sound effects strengthened by his contact with Heredia, he was to pursue Mallarmé's example further along his own line of development in which the sonnet will become something more subtly and musically psychological than it was in *Les Trophées*. Heredia was an important influence at a formative stage.[18]

Translations of *Les Trophées*, whole or in part, have appeared in many languages and often several in the same language: German, English, Spanish, Greek, Japanese, Norwegian, Polish, Rumanian, Russian, Serbian, Czech.[19] Though Heredia's fame and knowledge of his poetry were widely diffused by these translations, it is worth noting that among creative writers after 1890 Heredia does not seem to have left many explicit traces. In this country, for instance, the letters and essays of Yeats, Wilde and Lionel Johnson yield nothing. There is one reference in the correspondence of Ernest Dowson, in 1893, when he quotes 'Antoine et Cléopâtre' and describes it as 'very superb'. Ezra Pound and T. S. Eliot were well acquainted with the poetry of the late French nineteenth century but they record no impressions of Heredia; nor do the 'Rhymers' of the 1890s who showed much interest in Verlaine and Mallarmé. The passage we quote from the influential book on Symbolism by Arthur Symons (see p. 128) spoke for many in this country. Does one conclude that Heredia and perhaps Parnassian poetry generally was culturally inaccessible to the British or that Heredia's values were so classical that he did not capture the interest of British writers excited by the novel possibilities as well as the inherent worth of the more fashionable Verlaine? Or would it be true to say that *Les Trophées* are so dependent on the intrinsic pleasure to be derived from the way the French language is handled that Heredia did not easily cross the Channel? This would seem not to be the case because, we have already noted, Heredia soon became an admired classic of anthologies in this country and his position has been similar in many parts of the world. As we briefly noted earlier in this chapter, many of the younger and foremost creative spirits of the age, not just in Britain and France but in Europe, were to turn away from the traditions and examples of the past which had helped to form Heredia.

In Spanish-speaking countries his following has always been considerable. We must be careful not to confuse our poet, as some have done, with his homonymic cousin, born in Santiago de Cuba in 1803, whose high reputation among Spanish Americans is founded on his collection *Poesías* (New York, 1925). He was a very different poet from our José-Maria: openly passionate and committed to causes, like the freedom of Cuba, from which he was expelled for life for the promotion of his views. He died in Mexico in 1839. To this cousin, the French José-Maria wrote in 1903 three sonnets in Spanish (see *P.C.*, pp. 288–90) which were published in *El Fígaro* of Havana in the same year. Our own

Heredia's death was reported in detail by many Spanish newspapers in Havana at the end of October and during November in 1905, with various recapitulations of his greatness—*La Discusión*, the *Ateneo de la Habana*, the *Diario de la Marina* and *La Lucha*. Heredia was clearly thought to have deserved well of his native island. The difficulties of translating *Les Trophées* into Spanish were examined in *La Discusión* of 12 November 1905 and translations were offered of some sonnets by a number of writers. The articles in Paris in 1925 following the inauguration of Heredia's bust in the Luxembourg gardens were echoed in Cuba by No. 22 of the *Diario de la Marina* under the heading 'Paris honra al Poeta José-Maria de Heredia'. One of the early translators into Spanish of some of Heredia's sonnets, Max Henriquez Ureña, produced his complete, annotated, translation of *Les Trophées* many years later (see Bibliography). The fact that the translation appeared in Buenos Aires, in 1954, and yet another, complete and annotated, by José Antonio Niño, in Mexico, in 1957 (see Bibliography), is testimony to the continuing importance attached to Heredia's poetry in South America.

Heredia has remained an important landmark, the most accomplished representative of *Le Parnasse*, a classic absorbed not only by the French in France and those familiar with French poetry in any country but by those who have come under enough French influence in those areas of the world that formed part of France's colonial empire. The following sonnet, with impeccably regular rhymes, was composed by a poet from Guadeloupe, Gilbert de Chambertrand, and published in 1937:

> Midi! L'air qui flamboie, et brûle, et se consume
> Verse à nos faibles yeux l'implacable clarté.
> Tout vibre dans l'espace et sur l'immensité;
> L'azur est sans nuage et l'horizon sans brume.
>
> Là-bas, sur les récifs lointains frangés d'écume,
> Dans un grondement sourd par l'écho répété,
> La mer éclate et gicle au chaud soleil d'été,
> Et sur le flot mouvant chaque crête s'allume.
>
> Parfois, au bord du ciel et de l'océan bleu,
> On croit apercevoir sous l'atmosphère en feu
> Le contour d'une voile immobile et brillante . . .

Et sur la plage d'or, les sveltes cocotiers,
Dressant leurs fûts étroits dans l'heure étincelante,
Ont toute une ombre épaisse écrasée à leurs pieds.[20]

The memory of Leconte de Lisle is strong here and Baudelaire is not far away, but the influence of Heredia is combined with that of the older poets, in the theme, the strongly visual approach and the firm *facture*. In the book where I found this sonnet quoted, Chambertrand and others are stigmatized for their embodiment of the alien, metropolitan values of France, for writing in a manner that was current a hundred years ago, for not promoting or at least not showing awareness of *négritude*. Perhaps Chambertrand was a political innocent who simply loved Parnassian poetry. It is in such examples that Heredia's influence can still be detected as a creative force, however attenuated.

V

AN EVALUATION

Heredia's reputation rests on the sonnets of *Les Trophées*. His translations from the Spanish, particularly of Bernal Díaz, were a considerable achievement fully recognized in his time but if he had been the author of those alone, he would be scarcely remembered and certainly would not occupy the place, now generally acknowledged, of a minor classic, one of the finest and most representative of the Parnassian poets who better than any of them, not excepting Leconte de Lisle, combined Romantic ardour with precise powers of evocative suggestion. His virtues as a poet have been examined in some detail in my second and fourth chapters; the objectivity I have tried to achieve will not have masked my personal affection and admiration for the sonnets. In the present chapter's brief evaluation, we can perhaps most usefully explore the implications of several reservations mentioned in Chapter IV.

No French poet is now read mainly for his ideas. In a reasonably long historical perspective, our present expectation when reading poetry is a recent development. Even in the nineteenth century, French poets gave their views, told stories and recounted events almost as much as they sought to be lyrical, imaginative or ecstatic. In centuries before the nineteenth, epic poetry combined the two roles especially well and in the nineteenth century Lamartine and Hugo made valiant attempts to keep the epic alive. But the large epic vision was fading in the second half of the century as the Parnassians sought more compactness and precision and the Symbolists concentrated more on the inner soulscape. In the second half of the twentieth century, we are aware of the increasing separation of language's functions: on the one hand, the heightened apprehensions of the poet's imaginative feeling, on the other, the thin diet of the popular novel, the lifeless abstractions of administrative prose, the bland, silky and euphemistic half-truths of advertising or the taut, rational assessment of good analysis. More direct and more powerful stimuli than those given by language have been increasingly sought. Poetry is perhaps a less natural, less popular medium for the pleasure of writer or reader than ever it was. When the visual now predominates, it is less the written than the televisual. What then can we say to the occasional reproach, made more at the turn of the century than now, that *Les Trophées* lack 'thought'? In the first place, we can interpret it. It partly amounts to regretting that Heredia avoids any explicit intrusion of his own opinions in his sonnets. We noted in Chapter IV that his poetry became more out of tune with the prevailing attitudes of new poets after the end of the First World War. He literally had nothing to say by way of wanting to convince the reader of the rightness of particular views. He was neither oracular nor oneiric. His settled view of human nature, his espousal of Parnassian attitudes in poetry help us to understand why, unlike Rimbaud, still more unlike the later Surrealists, he did not want to 'changer la vie' by means artistic, metaphysical or political. What is for some modern readers a grave drawback is for others a blessed relief.

The past, and often the very distant past, bulks large in all Heredia wrote. This can be another barrier for the contemporary reader and in different ways. The knowledge of Greece and Rome or of medieval and Renaissance times, the whole classical background to much of *Les Trophées* which, until fifty or more years ago, formed part of the culture of many educated people in Western Europe is now confined to a very few, to what I suppose may be called an élite, when even universities have to abandon the study with their students of Latin and Greek poetry in the original because there are not enough applicants sufficiently versed in the two languages. The modern democrat may reflect that even a hundred years ago, the much larger proportion who had this classical culture still constituted an élite able to indulge its involvement in the past only at the expense of the millions who toiled or spun. For the majority of Frenchmen even in Heredia's time the background culture of much Parnassian poetry was a serious barrier. For the Parnassians themselves, this fact was not a matter of concern but of pride and pleasure. In our own times, the elitist quality of *Les Trophées* is even more keenly apparent than it used to be. Reserve, elitism, aristocratic or patrician tastes: it would take some time to assemble a list of values more alien in the contemporary world.

It can be further argued that much else in Heredia's attitude to the past is calculated to make the modern reader inimical or indifferent to his poetry. Not only are we now more hostile or indifferent to the traditional, not only are we tensed over the present or the near future, we are less sympathetic than past ages to both the epic and the heroic. As we read the sonnets in the subsection 'Les Conquérants' of 'Le Moyen Age et la Renaissance' or the history by Bernal Díaz of the conquest of New Spain, we risk missing what Heredia was trying to capture by thinking of the racial oppression of the Aztecs or the capitalistic greed of the *conquistadores* as

> Ils allaient conquérir le fabuleux métal
> Que Cipango mûrit dans ses mines lointaines.

That the Aztecs were brutally invaded and their civilization destroyed or that the Spanish explorers were greedy is certain. Do we therefore conclude that moral values have so changed since their and Heredia's day that we must regard such poetry as fatally flawed? Or do we try by an act of imagination to transport ourselves to their viewpoints? Or do we try to reach a compassionate, understanding synthesis of these two extremes as our attention is drawn to the aesthetic qualities involved? But the appreciation of the heroic raises a more general question in our age. Will Heredia perhaps attract readers all the more because the opportunities for the heroic have been diminished in our more industrialized, bureaucratized society? There is a seeming paradox in Heredia: he is drawn by the heroic in past civilizations yet he is not affected by what some would regard as the modern poet's equivalent of the heroic—his individual, often solitary, quest for originality, a frequently metaphysical quest which emerged from Romantic theory and practice and has grown ever more fiercely demanding in all artists since, poets, painters, sculptors or musicians. The paradox is soon resolved. The essential difference between Heredia's viewpoint and that of our day is that his nature is accepting and turns exuberantly to the world outside him: if my readers will permit an immense generalization, the spirit of our age is more prone to question and challenge than to accept and it is much more introspectively and often anxiously preoccupied with its own workings and with egalitarian morality than either Heredia or many of his contemporaries. Though as a writer he is of course more self-critical and reticent than Paul Claudel and shows no enthusiasm for Christianity, he has something of what Claudel envisaged as the poet's traditional capacity for *louange*. His 'âme d'un enfant' (see p. 26) was open, predominantly absorptive and receptive; it predisposed him to a sense of wonder and a love of the epic and heroic. His critical faculties were severe during the actual composition of his sonnets but they mainly served to sharpen his generous appeal to those expansive, imaginative powers, visual, rhythmic and aural, which lead us out of ourselves to the grateful acceptance and cele-bration of the world's splendours. For those readers who can appreciate it, this is the glory of *Les Trophées*: a sumptuous, visual and aural feast of the imagination.

Originality or newness for its own sake was not then one of Heredia's main concerns. When we say that he was classical in taste or manner, we imply not only that he inherited themes from masters like Catullus and the sonnet form from Ronsard and Chénier, but that he was happy to be so influenced and to follow models he loved and admired. He did make his mark with some new themes—most notably that of 'Les Conquérants'—and brought the evocative, dramatic powers of the sonnet to a pitch of authentic cogency which, when all predecessors have been acknowledged, stamps his manner and range of effects as *sui generis*. But his absorption of classical values makes his poetry as precarious now as the disappearing classical culture to which I have referred. What we now understand by 'poetry' incor-porates such a fondness for the spontaneous and the disparate that we regard as poetry lines like the following:

> I'm running
> Because when I am asleep
> The moon wakes my hair up
> That's why I'm running.

The sublunary image of hair being wakened up is in the spirit of much French poetry written since the 1920s. That the lines quoted were composed by a child of two years, though incidental, doubtless adds to their piquancy and perhaps to their authenticity and worth. She was saluted in the Times Diary of 29 September

1969 as 'possibly the youngest poet ever to appear in print'. Heredia could not have published such lines. More narrowly, the use of adjectives will briefly illustrate my point. Modern eyes are accustomed to the strange, daringly irrational or excitingly new epithets found by a Rimbaud to grasp his iconoclastic visions, deliberately provoked by Surrealist 'games' or tensely expelled by a René Char to cut through the accretions of habitual thinking and embody the sibylline simplicity of his central experience of life. We do find in *Les Trophées* adjectives that are original and startling, or that seem to forge new combinations with nouns— 'un monstrueux héros' ('Némée', l. 14, in 'La Grèce et la Sicile'), 'nuage effarouché' ('Stymphale', l. 9, in 'La Grèce et la Sicile'), 'la mouvante nuit' ('Pan', l. 8, in 'La Grèce et la Sicile'), 'la gueule glauque, innombrable et mouvante' ('Andromède au monstre', l. 8, in 'La Grèce et la Sicile'), 'cet ivoire souple' ('Vélin doré', l. 9, in 'Le Moyen Age et la Renaissance'), 'le glauque hippocampe' ('Email', l. 8, in 'Le Moyen Age et la Renaissance'). But really novel adjectives are in the minority. Many of Heredia's adjectives are classical in that, like some of Baudelaire's, they do not surprise, they are not intended to surprise; on the contrary, they are to some extent reassuringly expectable and strengthen the impression conveyed by other words in the line or clause of poetry. In 'Tel, nu, sordide, affreux, nourri des plus vils mets' ('L'Esclave', in 'La Grèce et la Sicile') the words 'nu', 'sordide', 'affreux' and 'vils' are mutually supporting parts of a dominant, harmonious impression. The slave has left 'l'île heureuse' (l. 5)—hypallage, perhaps, but whatever figure of speech we see it as, it reinforces the total picture of a harmoniously happy Sicily sharply contrasted with a harmoniously abject and unhappy slave. The eyes of the loved one left behind are 'purs': for some readers a banal adjective, for others, a spiritually comforting one and part of the contrast between past happiness and present distress. Similar remarks could be made concerning the adjectives in other sonnets, like the 'âcres parfums', 'feuilles mortes' and 'le choc avait été très rude' of 'Soir de bataille' ('Rome et les Barbares'). Pleonasm or near-pleonasm and circumlocution are features of the sonnets, which reveal what Gustave Kahn called 'de beaux dons d'éloquence continue': in many of them, a mostly untroubled, unintrospective and—by some modern standards—a doubtlessly simplistic dramatic speaker imparts a vision, a memory, an apostrophe to someone or something in language which relies for its force on rich description and predictable dramatic enumeration or climax. Ronsard and Du Bellay's sonnets often did much the same. As he celebrates the magnificence of history or art and the universal pageant of man, with all the constraints of his sonnet form, Heredia displays a lofty, grandiloquent ease whose whole rhythm and effects now seem lavishly leisured. Like most Renaissance poets and those of antiquity whose confidence in the world and in themselves extended to their use of language, Heredia set great store by his visible mastery of language. There is present in every aspect of his sonnets a degree of reflective contemplation, rational control and measured effects of symmetry, harmony and dissonance which for some contemporary tastes is old-fashioned and disagreeable. Verlaine called such writing *littérature* and more savage descriptions have been given it since. It is too naïvely assumed in our time that poetry which does not give the impression of being oracularly disordered must lack feeling and 'sincerity'. It is less appreciated than it once was that art can be more cogent when emotion and imagination find expression only after uniting in tension with intellectual strength and rational order. As readers of French poetry and without fearing we will become irresponsible aesthetes, we can share Verlaine's other view that 'toute forme est bonne du moment qu'elle est belle' and give ourselves the pleasure of enjoying both Heredia's more or less classical art and the superbly exciting freedom of much twentieth-century poetry.

But the importance of Heredia's attachment to the past should not be exaggerated. Though it has been used for hundreds of years, the sonnet form is well suited to modern sensibilities. It was no accident that there were so many sonnets in *Les Fleurs du mal*. Baudelaire became the apostle of *modernité*, he espoused Edgar Allan Poe's aesthetic viewpoint concerning the relation in modern times between brevity and intensity of poetic effect. He believed that if the current of poetic *enthousiasme* or what he called its *enlèvement de l'âme* is to pass into the reader, the poem must not be too long or the current will necessarily fade. Long epic poems cease to be poetic in the proper sense of the adjective.

Since Baudelaire's day the tendency has grown much stronger to prize intensity and brevity in poetry and other arts. In this respect, Heredia could scarcely be more modern. We have seen that in a form which by its limited scale compels the poet to be tellingly brief, he made Chénier and Leconte de Lisle seem by comparison quite prolix as he developed to the utmost every aspect of compactness and dramatic immediacy. With the possible exception of 'Les Conquérants de l'or' and his 'Roman-cero', the traditional *longueurs* of the epic are entirely rejected: fourteen lines have to embody what previous generations of poets expressed in hundreds. The epic, inherently exciting and potentially gripping, is therefore given greater intensity and powerful prolongations by Heredia's manner. The aura of expanding suggestion which is found particularly in the last lines of many sonnets brought him close to Symbolist tastes or to Baudelaire's predilection for 'l'expansion des choses infinies' ('Correspondances', *Les Fleurs du mal*). Heredia complements the precision of the Parnassians with the suggestion of the Sym-bolists: his marked fusion of the two traits is unique. Were it not for all the other traditional qualities in *Les Trophées*, Heredia would by these aspects alone be the most immediately appealing of poets. Radiant brevity is the soul of his sonnets.

But for some tastes the sonnet is too tight and cramped a form. Barbey d'Aurevilly wrote in 1889 of its 'petites difficultés vain-cues,' of 'cette forme essentiellement parnassienne du sonnet, [. . .] cette œuvre d'asthmatique qui, entre deux toux, place nettement son petit mot'.[1] The image is witty, but it tells us more about d'Aurevilly than about the sonnet. If some readers like only larger and freer forms, the wisest counsel to them is doubtless not to look at any more sonnets, certainly by Heredia, perhaps by any poet. D'Aurevilly was simply not equipped to see Heredia's worth. His mastery of the form, his 'virtuosity', incurs unfavour-able comment from those who, like d'Aurevilly, prefer less constrained verse-forms and usually a wider and deeper involve-ment in a greater range of themes and styles. Such controlled concentration by Heredia on the aesthetic power of words and rhythms in order to match the beautiful or the exhilarating he encountered in history or in art does not appeal to many readers. The limitations of *Les Trophées* are real and easily summarized.

However strong their aesthetic appeal, the sonnets largely exclude much in life that is central to most people, such as commitment to religion or a transcendent cause other than art itself or a deeper sense of the grandeur and pathos of lived human relationships. Heredia achieves his classical, heraldic beauty at a certain cost. There is a sameness not only in the perpetual quest for the significantly heroic and classically beautiful, not just in the detached posture of the poet who, with all his dramatic immediacy, takes the classically long view of human affairs but in the range of theatrical effects which is never great enough to prevent us sensing their predictability. Predictability was part of the classical canon: today it often bores. The consequence is that *Les Trophées* can give an impression of monotony which, however unfair and inaccurate in view of the real variety in the collection, remains in the reader's mind and doubtless accounts in part for Heredia's final consignment to anthologies.

Anyone reading too many of Heredia's sonnets at one time may tire of what Edmund Gosse neatly called his 'uniform strenuousness'. By other poets' standards, Verlaine's or Laforgue's, for example, Heredia is always trying very hard and his art is particularly concentrated. Even before the First World War there were lovers of poetry who preferred to Heredia's controlled, traditional and magniloquent perfection not just Verlaine's more casual and suggestive 'sincerity' but also Apollinaire's eclectic fusion of themes and tones. In such readers, the self-addressed reflection of Apollinaire's poem 'Zone' (1912, published in the collection *Alcools* of 1913)—'Tu en as assez de vivre dans l'antiquité grecque et romaine'—must have struck an answering chord. But we do not have to read through *Les Trophées* at one go, for the first or any subsequent time. How often do we do this for *recueils* by other poets? The unity for Heredia is the individual sonnet or at the most a subsection or section. The poems are not all epiphanies or ecstasies and we can balance the sonorous intensity of 'Bacchanale' ('La Grèce et la Sicile') or 'Soir de bataille' ('Rome et les Barbares') with the delicate pathos of 'La Prière du mort' ('La Grèce et la Sicile'), the comic joviality of 'Hortorum Deus III' ('Rome et les Barbares'), the comfortable domesticity of 'Hortorum Deus IV' or the rich Titian colouring of 'La Dogaresse' ('Le Moyen Age et la Renaissance'). Every poet worthy of his calling genuinely gives us what has affected him. The relative rarity of Heredia's consummately cultivated genius is his strength and his attraction. His poetry is a refined luxury, resolutely removed from the workaday. He can perhaps appeal most to those of our young in our modern world who are starved of truly organized and enduring beauty and to whom he is capable of serving as a fine example of a certain kind of poetry and an introduction to the linguistic and artistic resources deployed by a virtuoso; he will almost certainly occupy a less important if still cherished place in their affections as such readers' horizons broaden and they deepen their acquaintance with the wider-ranging or more complex art of, say, Baudelaire, Rimbaud, Mallarmé and Valéry. Heredia is a poet to whom those who know and love the greatest figures in French poetry can return without disappointment for delectation that is absorbing, unhurried and intellectually satisfying. He is worth our attention because he is not too like the mighty, fecund and usually longer-winded Hugo and different again from the musically protean Verlaine or the piercingly simple Eluard. Truly himself, he does supremely well what he sought to do: this he summed up with characteristically controlled enthusiasm when he reviewed Edouard de Beaumont's *La Fleur des belles épées* (1886), a kind of anthology of beautiful swords, with good reproductions. The talent he attributed to Beaumont is also his own:

Le don d'évocation est peut-être, de toutes les facultés de l'esprit, la plus merveilleuse. Ressusciter par la pensée, en un instant, grâce à de belles formes qui charment les yeux, un passé de gloire, d'amour, de batailles et de triomphes, toute une aventure héroïque, pompeuse, galante ou tragique, est-il, pour le Curieux, de plus exquise jouissance?[2]

The virtuosity with which Georges Pellissier in 1898 was reproaching Heredia is in fact his greatest glory. There is in *Les Trophées* an unfailing sense of craftsmanship, found in *objets d'art* and recreated in the handling of the sonnet. Craftsmanship is workmanship: for a sonnet by Heredia we feel something akin to the admiration and affection we accord to the traditional competence of a good carpenter or potter. It is this *facture*, so constant a concern of Parnassian poets, that, with all the other qualities of Heredia's sonnets, enables them to enshrine for each individual reader Heredia's own artistic pleasure and to become the poetic talismans which renew and prolong that pleasure each time we experience them. We may thus apply to Heredia himself the eulogy he composed for Gautier in his poem 'Monument' (*Le Tombeau de Théophile Gautier*, 1873):

> Car ses mains ont dressé le monument superbe
> A l'abri de la foudre, à l'abri du canon:
> Il l'a taillé dans l'or harmonieux du Verbe.

Poets do not have to be graded and perhaps cannot be. If Heredia must be assigned a place, that of minor classic may be the least unsatisfactorily arbitrary. Edmund Gosse went to the heart of the matter in 1894 when he wrote: 'To call José-Maria de Heredia a great poet would be to misuse language. He lacks the breadth and humanity of the leaders of poetry. But, beyond all question, he is a great poetic artist'. Gosse wisely joined what Georges Pellissier later split into *artiste* and *poète* when he affirmed that Heredia was rather the first than the second. 'Great poetic artist' will do. Heredia would have been quite content with that honourable definition.

VI

SOME VIEWS OF HEREDIA

Chez lui, au lieu de la rêverie harmonieuse, toute la robustesse avec un fracas de métal, et au lieu de teintes crépusculaires, le flamboiement aveuglant de midi.

La fureur rouge des cactus, le resplendissement des incendies nocturnes, l'azur vert du ciel persan et les pourpres et les ors de Paul Véronèse ou de Delacroix, n'ont que des teintes pâles, en regard des strophes éclatantes de José-Maria de Heredia. Ne lui demandez pas la grâce familière de François Coppée ni la philosophie subtile de Sully Prudhomme. Né sous le ciel chaud de Cuba, ce qui lui plaît et ce qu'il vous offre, ce sont de farouches floraisons de couleurs.

> Catulle Mendès, *La Légende du 'Parnasse contemporain'*, Bruxelles, Auguste Brancart, 1884, p. 258.

Or, tandis que d'autres donnaient dans le mysticisme sensuel de Baudelaire ou dans le bouddhisme de Leconte de Lisle, et tandis que presque tous étaient profondément tristes, le sentiment que M. José-Maria de Heredia exprimait de préférence, c'était je ne sais quelle joie héroïque de vivre par l'imagination à travers la nature et l'histoire magnifiées et glorifiées. En cela il se rencontrait avec M. Théodore de Banville; mais ce qui peut-être le distinguait entre tous, c'était la recherche de l'extrême précision dans l'extrême splendeur. Il joignait à l'ivresse des sons et des couleurs le goût d'une forme dont la brièveté, l'exactitude et la plénitude rappelassent en quelque façon nos écrivains classiques. Il rêvait d'enfermer un monde d'images dans un petit nombre de vers absolument parfaits, et de faire tenir les songes d'un dieu dans de petites coupes bien ciselées.

> Jules Lemaître, 'José-Maria de Heredia', *Les Contemporains, études et portraits littéraires* (2ème série), Paris, Boivin, 1886, p. 54.

D'un rêve d'or et de sang, bellement théâtral, il a fait des poèmes sans pensées et pleins de mouvement et de couleur, des vers sonores et rudes.

> Charles Morice, *La littérature de tout à l'heure*, Paris, Perrin, 1889, p. 219.

A Heredia [. . .], à lui, bien à lui, rien qu'à lui, l'ordonnance admirable, l'unité rigoureuse de chacun de ses petits poèmes, petits par la dimension, grands pour l'idée et l'image contenues, à lui le ton constamment noble et tendu dans la noblesse, tendu de la bonne sorte, inaccessible à quelque vulgarité que ce soit, à n'importe quelle faiblesse de style, ou concession de son rythme carré, de sa rime opulente et du mouvement comme militaire de ses périodes directes, légères, mais pleines, surtout, et j'y reviens, l'héroïsme ataval! de la pensée et de la vision.

Paul Verlaine, 'José-Maria de Heredia', *Les Hommes d'aujourd'hui*, *Œuvres en prose complètes*, Gallimard, Bibliothèque de la Pléiade, 1972, pp. 866–7 (original publication in 1892).

Il y a une méthode de travail, et, derrière cette méthode, une doctrine d'art. [. . .] Elle consiste à réconcilier la science et la poésie en n'arrivant à la seconde qu'à travers la première.

Paul Bourget, 'Science et poésie: à propos des *Trophées*', *Essais de psychologie contemporaine*, ii, Paris, Plon, 1926, p. 125 (originally published in 1893).

Contours des figures, mouvement des draperies, colorations, jeux de la lumière, il a tout saisi, tout fixé. Ce qui est caché aux yeux ne l'intéresse guère et le mystère des âmes ne le trouble point. Ce n'est pas qu'il manque d'émotion ni même parfois d'une sorte de mélancolie.

Anatole France, *La Vie littéraire*, (3ème série), Calmann-Lévy, 1893, p. 297.

Ce que je reproche à M. de Heredia, comme à tous les rajeunisseurs de légendes, c'est l'indifférence quiète et tranquille qu'il affecta en ces temps mauvais. Quant à ses vers, qui ne sont que des musiques ou des tableaux, si merveilleux qu'ils puissent nous paraître, ils seront vite oubliés de ceux qu'intéresse et inquiète la vie d'aujourd'hui et de demain, la seule vie. Qui n'atteignit point leur âme ne sera jamais des leurs.

Ludovic Hamilo, *L'Evénement*, 8 March 1894.

Le sonnet, tel que l'a exécuté José-Maria de Heredia, n'a plus rien de commun avec l'ancien sonnet de nos poètes et peut passer pour une chose absolument neuve dans notre langue. Au lieu d'une poésie d'idées, nous avons une poésie d'images. Plus de compliment, mais une peinture. On admirait des pensées; on voit un tableau. D'un côté, du dessin léger; de l'autre, de la couleur en relief. Le sonnet de Heredia est une superposition d'images accumulant leur effet sur la dernière; ce n'est plus même de la peinture: c'est de la sculpture.

> Antoine Albalat, 'José-Maria de Heredia et la poésie contemporaine', *La Nouvelle Revue*, 1 December 1894.

Impressions de joie, pures sensations d'art: c'est ce que nous offrent aujourd'hui les *Trophées*, et c'est ce que nous ne trouvons dans aucune autre œuvre moderne, sauf peut-être dans Théodore de Banville [. . .]

La recherche de la forme [. . .] est sereine et calme, elle a la tranquillité du marbre dont la blancheur uniforme éternise les frémissements de la chair; elle est l'incarnation du rêve joyeux de l'art parfait, du sourire de l'artiste qui a bien travaillé et se repose de son effort dans la contemplation de son œuvre [. . .]

M. de Heredia n'aime point les ombres et les ténèbres: il est l'amant du plein soleil et de la lumière crue. C'est, dans ses vers, un continu flamboiement de chaude clarté, un ruissellement d'or fauve, une incandescence de couleurs éclatantes.

> Henry Bordeaux, *Ames modernes*, Perrin, 1895, pp. 137, 138 and 145.

Tous les sonnets qu'il fit gardèrent inaltérablement la structure du premier sonnet qu'il avait fait. Cent dix-huit fois il eut la patience de recommencer la même besogne rythmique et de chanter les héros de tous les âges sur le même air [. . .]

Tout versificateur qui ne tire pas de son propre fonds sa façon de penser et de dire est contraint, pour y suppléer, de recourir à l'imitation et, par suite, n'a plus rien à attendre que de son habileté de practicien. Tel est, à y bien regarder, le cas de M. de Heredia. La poésie, n'étant plus pour lui une effusion, se réduit à un admirable travail de style. Ne demandez donc à ses sonnets ni émotion ni profondeur pourvu qu'ils soient des chefs-d'œuvre de facture.

> Raoul Rosières, 'M. J.-M. de Heredia', *La Revue bleue*, 25 May 1895, pp. 643-4.

Son *chartisme* n'a pas nui—tant s'en faut—à son esthétique. Les triomphes de la Philologie l'ont émerveillé. Il a vu les profondeurs du passé magnifiquement illuminées par ces sciences très spéciales que le vulgaire ignore ou méprise, et qui sont d'admirables lampes de mineur: l'archéologie, l'épigraphie, la diplomatique. Il a compris que l'office et le bienfait de la littérature consistent surtout à ouvrir au public des trésors cachés, et à faire entrer dans le domaine de tous ce qui était auparavant l'exclusive propriété de quelques spécialistes volontiers jaloux. Il a puisé à des sources mystérieuses et nouvelles. Ce Parnassien est un moderne.

Gaston Deschamps, 'José-Maria de Heredia', *La Vie et les livres* (3ème série), Colin, 1896, pp. 35–6.

M. de Heredia la [perfection] réalise à chaque coup. Triplement poète, il l'est, comme peintre, par l'éclat du coloris, comme sculpteur, par le galbe des contours, comme musicien, par la richesse des sonorités et l'harmonie des rythmes. Tous les arts ont concouru à la suprême beauté de son œuvre.

Plus artiste que poète, au sens où les deux termes s'opposent, il a fait de la poésie un miracle de virtuosité. Il en a retranché toute tendresse, toute sympathie du cœur, toute inquiétude de l'esprit. La seule émotion qu'il lui ait permise est celle du beau. [...]

Tout en rendant à cet irréprochable artiste l'hommage d'une admiration que son seul tort est de fatiguer, on peut concevoir la poésie autrement. Pour les classiques et les Parnassiens, la poésie est de la prose plus stricte, une prose asservie aux règles. Chose curieuse, que notre romantisme avec toutes ses fantaisies et ses audaces ait abouti finalement au triomphe de la discipline. Un Malherbe flamboyant, voilà bien M. de Heredia.

Georges Pellissier, 'José-Maria de Heredia', *Etudes de littérature contemporaine*, i, Perrin, 1898, pp. 12–13.

Leconte de Lisle turned the world to stone, but saw, beyond the world, only a pause from misery in a Nirvana never subtilised to the Eastern ecstasy. And, with all these writers [Taine, Flaubert, Leconte de Lisle, Zola], form aimed above all things at being precise, at saying rather than suggesting, at saying what they had to say so completely that nothing remained over, which it might be the business of the reader to divine. And so they have expressed, finally, a certain aspect of the world; and some of them have carried style to a point beyond which the style that says, rather than suggests, cannot go. The whole of that movement comes to a splendid funeral in Heredia's sonnets, in which the literature of form says its last word, and dies.

> Arthur Symons, *The Symbolist Movement in Literature*, London, Constable, 1899, Introduction.

Son éclatante poésie semble moins reproduire la nature vivante que des pièces d'orfèvrerie. Chaque sonnet est comme un plat somptueux, où, dans un champ limité, la fantaisie d'un puissant artiste aurait enfermé des sujets historiques ou mythologiques. Ce maître ciseleur a réussi par la splendeur de son art: mais c'est un art qui n'est pas du tout dans le mouvement.

> Gustave Lanson, *Histoire de la littérature française*, 1902, p. 1107.

L'érudition, la langue et la rime s'unissent pour produire des effets surprenants; dédaigneux d'éloquence, exempts d'émotion, ces sonnets procurent le plaisir d'un art achevé; ils montent d'un jet pour s'élargir au dernier vers, d'un mouvement régulier, sans traits ni sautes brusques. Ils sont comme des bijoux faits de pierreries et d'or: ils en ont l'éclat un peu dur et le fini; ils sont décoratifs comme eux. C'est peut-être la perfection de la pure poésie parnassienne.

> Max Jasinski, *Histoire du sonnet en France*, Douai, Dalsheimer, 1903, p. 221.

Il continuait la grande tradition classique à prendre le mot dans sa large et vraie acception—André Chénier, et par lui Ronsard, et par Ronsard l'antiquité. [. . .]

Quant à son originalité, c'était son art du ramassé qui est brillant et qui reste clair, art où absolument personne ne l'a dépassé, ne l'a égalé peut-être.

> Emile Faguet, 'José-Maria de Heredia', *La Revue des poètes*, 10 October 1905.

Il est à noter qu'à l'apparition des *Trophées*, il n'y eut aucun article qui fut défavorable à l'œuvre; il y eut des dithyrambes, et nombreux, mais tout ce qui ne retentissait pas d'acclamations était plus que déférent. La stricte impartialité faisait un devoir de reconnaître à l'artiste le maniement suprêmement élégant d'une forme difficile, un élargissement considérable de cette forme fixe, une admirable qualité, la concision, de beaux dons d'éloquence

continue, un vaste répertoire de visions et de couleurs, une dé-
cision d'art qui ne laissait point au livre de pages faibles. C'est
beaucoup.

Gustave Kahn, 'José-Maria de Heredia', *La Revue*, 15 October
1905, p. 506.

There are no ethics in *Les Trophées*. Their subject is the world
of facts, not that of our explanations of these facts, or of our
attempts to find for ourselves rules for right conduct in dealing
with them. [. . .]
Life, as he sees it, is neither a school of morals nor a hothouse
of sentiment; what he sees in it is the most splendid of pageants
[. . .]
Nothing is more striking in these sonnets than the grand chords
on which they nearly always close. [. . .]
[. . .] the serenely ordered splendours, the processional magnificence, of José-Maria de Heredia.

John C. Bailey, *The Claims of French Poetry*, London, Constable,
1907, pp. 291, 293, 297 and 313.

Son œuvre n'est guère qu'une marqueterie dont les matériaux
ont été pris de tous côtés, mais groupés avec une science merveilleuse, dans une harmonie de tons consommée. [. . .]
Une des particularités les plus remarquables de l'art de de
[sic] Heredia, c'est que son travail sur les objets de sa vision et de
sa description les simplifie et les stylise jusqu'à les réduire à un
type d'une beauté en quelque sorte héraldique. Cette habitude le
conduit à des synthèses merveilleuses.

Eugène Langevin, 'José-Maria de Heredia—son œuvre poétique',
Le Correspondant, 10 January 1907, pp. 66–7 and 76.

Gourmont est tout à fait de mon avis que Coppée est autant un
'poète' que Heredia et Sully-Prudhomme ne le sont pas. Nous
nous sommes trouvés à le dire ensemble. Etre un homme de son
époque, décrire les choses, parler des choses de son époque, non
pas s'amuser à des reconstitutions grecques ou latines, c'est là le
vrai écrivain, le seul qui compte (5 June 1908). [. . .]
Plus loin, il [Valéry] rapporte un mot de Mallarmé à Degas,
mot qu'il semble bien approuver: *Ce n'est pas avec des idées qu'on
fait des vers. C'est avec des mots.* Ah! non, non, non. J'abomine ce
précepte littéraire. La littérature qui repose sur les mots? Aucun

intérêt. Heredia en est un bel exemple comme poète. Valéry, avec ses vers, en sera peut-être un autre, un jour (2 March 1938).

> Paul Léautaud, *Journal littéraire*, Mercure de France, ii. 1915, p. 225 and xii, 1962, p. 107.

Il existe en effet, entre l'épigramme et le sonnet, une affinité essentielle et très sensible; tous les deux sont le cadre idéal pour une poésie brève et resserrée, une forme qui s'adapte à merveille à l'expression concentrée d'une pensée ou d'un sentiment; tous les deux ont la même netteté et la même justesse, la même tendance à se terminer par une pointe.

> Emile Zilliacus, 'José-Maria de Heredia et *l'Anthologie grecque*', *Revue d'histoire littéraire de la France*, April—June 1910.

C'est en faisant de ses sonnets épigrammatiques de petits drames que le poète a su être très original alors qu'il imitait de près, et qu'il a pu mettre de l'unité dans des pièces faites de traits empruntés à des sources diverses.

> Joseph Vianey, 'Les Sonnets grecs de Heredia', *Revue des cours et conférences*, 29 June 1911, p. 771.

En somme, c'est dans cette alliance entre la large synthèse et l'exactitude minutieuse, que réside l'heureuse originalité de Heredia.

> René Pichon, 'L'Antiquité romaine et la poésie française à l'époque parnassienne', *Revue des deux mondes*, 1 September 1911, p. 150.

Je pense que le jour où on fera une édition critique des *Trophées*, où l'on comparera les premières et les dernières versions de ces sonnets *implacablement beaux*, on regrettera presque autant les corrections heureuses que les corrections maladroites. Verlaine nous a appris à aimer une certaine gaucherie et surtout un certain inachevé.

> Remy de Gourmont, 'M. de Heredia et les poètes parnassiens', *Promenades littéraires* (2ème série), Mercure de France, 1913, p. 51.

A relire les célèbres sonnets, on est frappé tout d'abord par ce qu'ils ont d'éclat, de couleur et de sonorité, mais, quand leur rumeur héroïque s'est apaisée, il me semble y entendre peu à peu une voix mélancolique et tendre. Leurs colorations vives et riches se nuancent de touches fines et sobres. A côté des concisions épiques se montrent des douceurs charmantes.

> Henri de Régnier, *Portraits et souvenirs*, Mercure de France, 1913, p. 70.

C'est donc en quelque sorte malgré lui, et comme à son insu, que Heredia se manifeste comme un poète élégiaque [. . .] Il y a en eux [ses sonnets] tant de couleur et de sonorité que la tristesse disparaît sous l'impression de splendeur et de vie qui s'en dégage. Si les grandes douleurs sont muettes, la mélancolie, pour se communiquer au lecteur, gagne à se traduire en notes plus voilées et moins éclatantes. Est-il rien, par exemple, qui soit d'une tristesse plus puissante que le sujet du sonnet liminaire de *l'Oubli*, tristesse puissante comme la mer évoquée par le dernier vers, mais tristesse visuelle pour ainsi dire, où la beauté des images et la fanfare des syllabes font tort à la sincérité de l'émotion.

Fernand Brodel, 'L'Elégie chez Heredia', *Mercure de France*, 15 August 1920, pp. 119–20.

On l'accuse à tort d'avoir poussé à l'extrême son souci de perfection, et on nous le montre comme un orfèvre qui s'amuse seulement à ciseler le métal et à polir l'émail. Il fut, au contraire, toujours et surtout un grand lyrique, non pas larmoyant et excessif à la manière des romantiques, mais sans cesse tourmenté par l'amour des belles choses et par un désir sans bornes.

Armand Goday, 'Le Poète des *Trophées* et l'Amérique', *Le Figaro*, Supplément littéraire, 17 October 1925, p. 2.

Car on ne l'a pas assez dit, et trop souvent les critiques de Heredia ont fait écho à Charles Morice: 'D'un rêve d'or et de sang, bellement théâtral, il a fait des poèmes sans pensée'. Mais les *Trophées* ne sont-ils pas un des plus beaux romans de l'humanité? Ils racontent l'histoire grandiose et douloureuse de l'homme, depuis ses luttes originelles avec la nature jusqu'à son ascension vers l'idéal de l'art et de la beauté. Heredia glorifie l'héroïsme et le génie, mais il célèbre aussi la leçon quotidienne de la tâche accomplie. Il accepte les lois de la nature, il chante la perpétuité des sentiments humains devant ses bienfaits et ses mystères. Et il en tire un stoïcisme moins amer que celui d'Alfred de Vigny, moins sombre que celui de Leconte de Lisle, une leçon d'acceptation plus sereine, un sentiment plus équilibré de la vie. Cette sérénité donne à son œuvre le charme suprême, celui d'apaiser l'âme.

Miodrag Ibrovac, *Journal des débats*, 18 October 1925, p. 1.

Soit qu'il s'inspire de l'antiquité gréco-romaine, soit qu'il évoque pour nous le Moyen Age ou la Renaissance, soit qu'il nous entraîne à la suite des Conquérants de l'Or, chacun de ses poèmes, chacun des vers et des mots rares qui les composent, par la richesse de leur substance et leur pouvoir de suggestion, trouvent des résonances multiples et lointaines au fond de nos esprits, parce que, tout en y remuant les joies esthétiques les plus pures, ils y réveillent aussi des souvenirs historiques et littéraires qui s'y étaient assoupis.

La composition des *Trophées*, œuvre de synthèse magistrale, suppose d'innombrables lectures et de fait Heredia fut un savant d'une très large culture.

> Jacques Guignard, 'A la Bibliothèque de l'Arsenal, le Centenaire de José-Maria de Heredia', *Sources—études, recherches, informations des Bibliothèques Nationales de France*, Bibliothèque Nationale, 1943, p. 117.

An orthodox 'parnassian' and a true aristocrat, Heredia avoided all mystery, all personal sources of inspiration, choosing only to deal with the loftiest subjects, sanctified by time. He knew nothing of the heart-rending torments of Baudelaire, Rimbaud and Verlaine; he discovered no kingdoms hitherto unknown to poetry; even more were the subtle researches of Mallarmé foreign to him. His prosody is strictly traditional. He seeks perfection solely in the domain of rich and flawless form and in the clear harmonies of felicitous language. His achievements in this field have kept his work alive.

> André Labarthe, *Poésies choisies de Stéphane Mallarmé et 'Les Trophées' de José-Maria de Heredia*, London, Barnard and Westwood, 1943, p. 100.

Or cet imagier a été aussi un assembleur de sons, ce phénix du Parnasse a montré un art du ramassé qui le rapproche de certains Symbolistes.

> Henri Clouard, *Histoire de la littérature française du symbolisme à nos jours*, Michel, 1947, p. 209.

NOTES

I. JOSE-MARIA DE HEREDIA

1. There is no justification for the acute accents which some writers put on the two *es* of his surname.

For many of the details that follow concerning Heredia's family I am indebted in the first place to Ibrovac who gleaned them from sources he indicates, including the family papers which I have consulted in the Bibliothèque de l'Institut.

2. Simone Szertics, *L'Héritage espagnol de José-Maria de Heredia*, Klincksieck, 1975, p. 13.

3. Bibliothèque de l'Institut under its own catalogue number: 11 (5679).

4. L. Barracand, 'Souvenirs des lettres', *La Revue de Paris*, 1 March 1914, p. 188.

5. 'Discours prononcé par le poète comme président du XXIXe banquet de l'Association amicale des anciens élèves de l'Institution de Saint-Vincent, à Paris, à l'Hôtel Continental', *Annuaire de l'Association amicale des anciens élèves de l'Institution de Saint-Vincent*, 1879, pp. 9–12. See Ibrovac, i, p. 24 for a long extract.

6. It seems that Ibrovac (i, p. 28) confuses Heredia's summer activities in 1856 with those of another year.

7. Ange Galdemar, 'L'Œuvre posthume de Leconte de Lisle, conversation avec M. de Heredia', *Le Gaulois*, 19 May 1895.

8. See Heredia's preface to the *Voyage en Patagonie* (Hachette, 1901) by the comte Henry de la Vaulx where he recalls that

> quelques jeunes hommes se rencontraient deux ou trois fois la semaine dans un petit rez-de-chaussée obscur et bas de la rue d'Amsterdam. C'était le bureau de rédaction de *La Revue française* [. . .] C'est là dans ce lieu sans lumière, que, pour la première fois, j'entendis le beau poète Armand Silvestre réciter ses premiers *Sonnets païens*, magnifiques et voluptueux. Jules Clarétie y fit ses premières armes de plume. Quant à moi, je confesse y avoir publié quelques médiocres sonnets, mal venus et mal bâtis, à rimes incorrectement entrecroisées, dont Théophile Gautier, avec sa bonhomie gouailleuse, paternelle et magistrale, daigna me dire: '—Comment! Si jeune, et tu fais déjà des sonnets *libertins*!'—Et c'est pourquoi je n'en fis et je n'en ferai plus jamais de tels.

9. 'Discours prononcé le 21 juillet 1894 aux funérailles de Leconte de Lisle', Institut de France, Académie française, Firmin-Didot, 1894, p. 8. Cf. Mendès: 'La seule discipline qu'il imposât,—c'était la bonne,—consistait dans la vénération de l'art, dans le dédain des succès faciles. Il était le bon conseiller des probités littéraires; sans gêner jamais l'élan personnel de nos aspirations divines, il fut, il est encore notre conscience poétique elle-même [. . .] Il condamne ou absout et nous sommes soumis' (*La Légende du 'Parnasse contemporain'*, Bruxelles, Brancart, 1884, p. 226). Cf. also Maurice Barrès: 'C'était une sorte de prêtre, qui dénonçait le siècle au nom du Beau éternel' ('Discours de réception à L'Académie française', Firmin-Didot, 1907, p. 12).

10. It was Barbey d'Aurevilly's scathing comments, in November 1866 in the *Nain jaune*, which did much to bring the Parnassian poets to the attention of a wide public.

11. Heredia is seen as recapturing some of the militant glory of the literary battles fought by the Romantics at the end of the 1820s.

12. A dig at Lamartine's famous poem 'Le Lac' (*Méditations poétiques*, 1820).

13. Quoted by U.-V. Châtelain, 'José-Maria de Heredia, sa vie et son milieu', *Cahiers des études littéraires françaises*, fascicule no. 2, undated, p. 6.

14. Cf. Gérard d'Houville, *Poésies*, Grasset, 1931, p. 182, for her poem 'Anniversaire' and the lines:

> O mon Père si beau, si charmant et si bon,
> Dont le cœur était fait d'une clarté si pure, [. . .]

15. The atmosphere in Heredia's family when his daughters were older is summed up by Gide in his *Journal 1889–1939*, Gallimard, 1951, p. 517: 'A table, on parle de la famille Heredia: milieu charmant, un peu bruyant, mais si amusant, si fantasque!' (12 November 1915).

16. Heredia's contacts outside France were very limited. He went to Spain and there were three visits to Italy, important for his appreciation of its art treasures, especially painting. (See the Athlone French Poets edition of *Les Trophées*, pp. 16–17). The first visit to Italy was in 1861 on a walking tour with two young friends, the second in 1864 with Georges Lafenestre and the third on his honeymoon in 1867.

17. See the article in the Bibliography by Joanna Richardson.

18. See the Bibliography for the various writings by Albalat, Barracand, Hanotaux, Lavagne and Régnier.

19. See the 'Discours prononcés dans la séance publique tenue par l'Académie française pour la réception de M. Maurice Barrès le jeudi 17 janvier 1907', Firmin-Didot, 1907, p. 26, where le vicomte Melchior de Vogüé recalls the time when he introduced Heredia to the Académie française and the speech that Heredia made:

L'ami qui l'assistait ne pouvait se défendre d'une inquiétude. N'allait-on pas sourire dans la salle, aux sonneries de ce clairon tumultueux et bégayant? Combien de gens avions-nous vus déçus, à une première audition de ses vers, par le marteleur de syllabes qui buttait sur l'hémistiche, hésitait, se cabrait devant la rime, comme si l'esprit cherchait encore cette rebelle, et soudain l'étreignait avec un rugissement de victoire! L'accoutumance aidant, on raffolait de l'originale diction; récités par une autre bouche, les sonnets nous paraissaient vidés d'une moitié de leur magnificence.

20. See the risqué anecdote, coming from Barbey d'Aurevilly, which Gide recalls that Heredia liked to quote, in *Journal 1889–1939*, Gallimard, 1951, p. 948 (23 October 1929).

21. Cf. Barracand, op. cit., p. 185: 'Il était très répandu et il recevait beaucoup. Il allait dans le monde, lui et les siens, figurait dans toutes les solennités et banquets littéraires'.

22. See Szertics, op. cit., p. 31.

23. See Albalat, 'Les "Samedis" de J.-M. de Heredia', *La Revue hebdomadaire*, 4 October 1919, p. 35.

24. 'Réponse au discours de réception à l'Académie française de M. de Heredia', Firmin-Didot, 1895, pp. 32 and 34. Cf. Langevin, 'José-Maria de Heredia', *Le Correspondant*, 10 January 1907, p. 81: 'Sa franche cordialité, la verve méridionale de sa causerie, sa familiarité qui savait rester distinguée, sont des traits qu'on n'oubliera pas.'

25. 'Discours prononcés dans la séance publique tenue par l'Académie française pour la réception de M. Maurice Barrès le jeudi 17 janvier 1907', Firmin-Didot, 1907, p. 14.

26. *Portraits et souvenirs*, Mercure de France, 1913, p. 68.

27. Albalat, op. cit., pp. 37 and 39.

28. Cf. Edmond et Jules de Goncourt, *Journal*, Les Editions de l'imprimerie nationale de Monaco, 1956, tome 21, 16 June 1895: 'Daudet me cite le mot de Huret, qui aurait dit tout joyeux: "Maintenant que Heredia est à l'Académie, nous saurons tout ce qui s'y passe!".'

29. See Barracand, op. cit., p. 184.

30. 'In Memoriam' in the book entitled *In Memoriam*, Librairie Henri Leclerc, 1906, p. 6.

31. *Contre Sainte-Beuve*, Gallimard, Bibliothèque de la Pléiade, 1971, pp. 221–2.

32. Thus, in a letter to Fauvelle's son Ernest on 26 November 1868, after discussing political events in Cuba, Spain and the U.S.A., he ends by begging pardon for 'cette longue tartine politique'. Writing to his mother from Menton on 28 April 1872–he had been there eighteen months, avoiding all the troubles in Paris at the time—he concludes: 'Quel cabanon de fous ou d'imbéciles que le monde!'.

33. Coppée, op. cit., p. 34.

34. 'José-Maria de Heredia', *Extrait des Mémoires de la Société Dunker-quoise*, Dunkerque, Imprimerie Paul Michel, 1906, p. 5.

35. See the 'Discours . . .' mentioned in note 19, p. 16, where Barrès speaks of Heredia's habits of composition: 'Il méditait longuement un sujet, il trouvait une image, un trait, un vers, puis un autre, qu'il notait. A haute voix, en se promenant, il ne se lassait pas de lire, pour en éprouver le son'.

II. THE POETRY

1. I am grateful to the Bibliothèque de l'Institut for permission to quote from the papers they hold.

2. See E. Díez-Canedo, 'Heredia y las influencias españolas', *Letras de América*, Mexico, 1944, p. 193 and Simone Szertics, op. cit., p. 154.

3. In a letter to José-Maria of 28 December 1860 Fauvelle proved to be rather preoccupied about the poem having too much *enjambement*!

4. See Ibrovac, i, p. 62.

5. See Szertics, op. cit., p. 157.

6. It contains too, in principle, the idea behind 'Fleurs de feu' (1866) and 'Fleur séculaire' (1876) in 'L'Orient et les tropiques'.

7. Manuscript in Bibliothèque de l'Institut.

8. Ibid.

9. Ibid.

10. The poems in *Les Contemplations* which I have in mind are in the first book, 'Aurore', like 'Lise', 'La Coccinelle' or 'Vieille Chanson du jeune temps'.

11. *Histoire de la conquête du Pérou, précédée d'un tableau de la civilisation des Incas*, traduite de l'anglais par H. Poret, Firmin-Didot, 1861. See Ibrovac, *Sources*, p. 170, and Szertics, op. cit., p. 167.

12. See Alison Fairlie, *Leconte de Lisle's Poems on the Barbarian Races*, O.U.P., 1947, p. 288.

13. The three poems by Leconte de Lisle to which reference has been made are all in his *Poèmes barbares* (1862). It is difficult to know which of the two poets was first in this field; see the interesting letter from Leconte de Lisle to Heredia, offering precise advice about 'Le Serrement de mains', in Ibrovac, i, p. 287.

14. Fairlie, op. cit., p. 314.

15. See the works by Asselineau and Jasinski in our Bibliography.

16. Cf. the two sonnets in 'Le Moyen Age et la Renaissance', 'Sur Le Livre des Amours de Pierre de Ronsard' and 'La Belle Viole'.

17. *Untersuchungen über den Aufbau, Reim und Stil der 'Trophées'*, Greifs-wald, 1913.

18. See the commentaries in our edition and also Chapter III below for Heredia's views on the alexandrine.

19. Cf. Chapter I, note 8.

20. 'Discours prononcé à l'inauguration de la statue de Joachim du Bellay, à Ancenis, le dimanche 2 septembre 1894,' Institut de France, Firmin-Didot, 1894, p. 6.

III. OTHER WORKS

1. Particularly 'Centaures et Lapithes' and 'Fuite de Centaures' in 'La Grèce et la Sicile'.

2. 'M. José-Maria de Heredia' in *La Littérature contemporaine. Opinions des écrivains de ce temps*, Mercure de France, 1905, pp. 283–8.

3. Henriette de Chizeray-Cuny, *Marie de Régnier (Gérard d'Houville): propos et souvenirs*, Les Presses de l'office mécanographique à Paris, 1969, p. 18.

4. Cf. Albalat, op. cit., p. 53: 'J'ai rarement entendu Heredia parler peinture, bien qu'il aimât les enluminures et les belles illustrations. En revanche, il méprisait franchement la musique. "C'est, disait-il, en parodiant un mot célèbre, le plus cher et le plus imprécis de tous les bruits. Le même air peut être à la fois un air de fête et une marche funèbre. La musique n'a que l'expression qu'on lui donne et dépend de la sensation de chacun. C'est un art inférieur, parce qu'il est *informulé*. Voyez *le Lac* de Lamartine. La poésie est belle. La musique en a fait une romance banale".'

5. Henri de Régnier, *Portraits et souvenirs*, Mercure de France, 1913, p. 49.

6. 'Discours de réception à l'Académie française', Lemerre, 1895, p. 21.

7. Ibid., p. 7.

8. 'Discours prononcé le 21 juillet 1894 aux funérailles de Leconte de Lisle', Institut de France, Académie française, Firmin-Didot, 1894, pp. 7–8.

9. Heredia's preface to Saint-Juirs, *Le Cabaret des trois vertus*, Tallandier, 1895.

10. 'Le Manuscript des *Bucoliques*', *La Revue des deux mondes*, 1 November 1905, p. 165.

11. Philippe Dufour, *Poèmes légendaires*, Lemerre, 1897, avec une lettre de José-Maria de Heredia.

12. 'Ernest Christophe', *Les Lettres et les arts*, 1 August 1886, pp. 203–4.

13. Cf., under 'Díaz del Castillo' in the Bibliography, the translation by Maudsley of the Spanish masterpiece as well as the edition by Cabañas which, on pp. ix-xxix, gives a transcription of the original

manuscript by Díaz, an account of its history and qualities and, pp. xxix-xxxiii, a list of editions and translations since Remón's edition (Madrid, 1632).

14. See the Cabañas edition of 1962 mentioned above in note 13.

15. There is a useful translation available for the modern reader: Bernal Díaz, *The Conquest of New Spain*, translated with an introduction by J. M. Cohen, Penguin Books, 1963. Cohen translates only the major part of Díaz's work, the first 157 chapters, leaving out chapters 158–214. He therefore covers the first three of Heredia's four volumes: but these are the most gripping and deal with the first entry into Mexico and its reconquest.

16. Cf. *Biblioteca de Autores Españoles desde la formación del lenguaje hasta nuestros días, Obras de Fernan Caballero*, Collección Rivadeneira, Ediciones Atlas, vol. v, Madrid, 1961.

17. The manuscripts in the Bibliothèque de l'Arsenal (13546) reveal the little progress Heredia apparently made in his translation of *Don Quixote*: just four pages, in his own handwriting, translating the first chapter.

IV. HEREDIA'S REPUTATION AND INFLUENCE

1. 'José-Maria de Heredia' in *Les Hommes d'aujourd'hui*, Verlaine, *Œuvres complètes*, Messein, 1926, p. 459.

2. Cf. A. Albalat, 'Les "Samedis" de J.-M. de Heredia', *La Revue hebdomadaire*, 4 October 1919, p. 60.

3. 'Au fracas des buccins qui sonnent leur fanfare dans le heurt de toutes sortes de cymbales et de gongs, tout savant qu'il est, on regrette parfois Verlaine et sa romance:

> Ecoutez la chanson bien douce,
> Elle est discrète, elle est légère:
> Un filet d'eau sur de la mousse.' (p.75)

4. This question is discussed in more detail in our edition, pp. 10–12.

5. Cf. his examination of 'Centaures et Lapithes' in our edition, p. 9.

6. See the Bibliography for the various writings by Hanotaux, Lavagne and Régnier as well as by Barracand and Albalat.

7. Baudelaire's sonnet 'Correspondances' in *Les Fleurs du mal* is doubtless better known than the Verlaine poem—'Clair de lune' in *Fêtes galantes*—which Brodel perhaps has in mind with his reference to 'mode mineur'.

8. For a few details concerning biography and literary history, Ibrovac's study needs to be complemented by Simone Szertics, *L'Héritage espagnol de José-Maria de Heredia*, Klincksieck, 1975.

9. See the *recueil de journaux, périodiques, coupures de presse et documents*

divers at the Bibliothèque de l'Arsenal in Paris, catalogued 4 N.F. 26006.

10. See also *An Anthology of Modern French Poetry 1850–1950*, selected and edited by Peter Broome and Graham Chesters, C.U.P., 1976, which has neither Leconte de Lisle nor Heredia.

11. It was through Heredia speaking of Samain to Brunetière that the latter got Samain into *La Revue des deux mondes*; see Georges Lecomte, 'Heredia au Luxembourg', *La Renaissance politique, littéraire, artistique*, 29 December 1923.

12. The article did not appear in *Le Courrier libre* and had to wait over fifty years before it was published by Henri Mondor in 'Le Premier Article de Paul Valéry', *Dossiers*, pp. 13–20, Janin, July 1946.

13. 'L'Esthétique valéryenne du sonnet', *Australian Journal of French Studies* vi (1969), p. 334.

14. 'Autres Rhumbs' in *Œuvres*, Gallimard, Bibliothèque de la Pléiade, ii, 1960, p. 676.

15. Hytier, op. cit., p. 330.

16. *Lettres à quelques-uns*, Gallimard, 1952, p. 42.

17. *Cahiers Paul Valéry: I. Poétique et Poésie*, Gallimard, 1975, pp. 26–7.

18. See my paper 'Valéry et Heredia' given at the *Colloque Valéry* held at the University of Edinburgh in November 1976. It is expected that all its proceedings will be published in one volume by Nizet in 1979.

19. See Ibrovac, ii, pp. 579–83 for further details.

20. Lilyan Kesteloot, *Les Ecrivains noirs de langue française: naissance d'une littérature*, Editions de l'Institut de Sociologie, Université libre de Bruxelles, 1971, pp. 37–8.

V. AN EVALUATION

1. Barbey d'Aurevilly, *XIXe siècle (2ème série): Les Œuvres et les hommes: les poètes*, Lemerre, 1889, p. 308.

2. *Les Lettres et les arts*, 1 June 1886, p. 135.

SELECT BIBLIOGRAPHY

Only writings which have been discussed or mentioned in this monograph are listed here. The order is alphabetical. Abbreviations of a few works to which frequent reference is made are given after the work. Paris can be assumed to be the place of publication for mentions of writings in French that do not specify place.

WORKS BY HEREDIA

Unpublished manuscripts, Bibliothèque Nationale, Bibliothèque de l'Arsenal and Bibliothèque de l'Institut, Paris.

Poetry

Poésies complètes de Heredia, Les Trophées, sonnets et poèmes divers, texte définitif avec notes et variantes, Lemerre, 1924 (*P.C.*). For the poetry, this edition is comprehensive; it gives all the poems published during Heredia's life and those that were published between his death and 1924. It can be usefully complemented by Szertics' book (see below).

Les Trophées, edited by W. N. Ince, 'Athlone French Poets', The Athlone Press, 1979. This critical edition appears as a companion to the present volume. The text is that of the first edition, Lemerre, 1893 (with the omission of 'Romancero' and 'Les Conquérants de l'or').

Details of the various editions of *Les Trophées*, including luxury editions that appeared after the first edition may be consulted in Ibrovac, i, pp. 578–9. No editions of importance have appeared since Ibrovac's thesis in 1923 save two usefully annotated editions, in Spanish, which are *Los Trofeos*, edited by José Antonio Niño, Universidad Nacional Autónoma de Mexico, 1957, and *Los Trofeos (Sonetos)*, edited by Max Henriquez Ureña, Biblioteca Contemporánea, Editorial Losada, Buenos Aires, 1954.

Correspondence

Many letters are quoted in Ibrovac, i. Others quoted in this monograph are from the unpublished manuscripts in the Bibliothèque de l'Institut, Paris.

Translations by Heredia

Véridique Histoire de la conquête de la Nouvelle Espagne, par le capitaine Bernal Díaz del Castillo, l'un des Conquérants, traduite de l'espagnol, avec une introduction et des notes, par José-Maria de Heredia, Lemerre, 4 vols, 1877–87.

Juan Soldado, conte andalou, librement traduit d'un des *Cuentos populares*, publiés par F. Caballero, *Journal des débats*, 1 January 1885.

La Nonne Alferez, illustrations de Daniel Vierge, gravées par Privat-Richard, Lemerre, 1894.

Other Writings
(mostly speeches and prefaces)

'Discours prononcé par le poète comme président du XXIXe banquet de l'Association amicale des anciens élèves de l'Institution de Saint-Vincent, à Paris, à l'Hôtel Continental', *Annuaire de l'Association amicale des anciens élèves de l'Institution de Saint-Vincent, 1879*, pp. 9–12.

'Ernest Christophe', *Les Lettres et les arts*, 1 August 1886, pp. 198–204.

'Discours prononcé le 21 juillet 1894 aux funérailles de Leconte de Lisle', Institut de France, Académie française, Firmin-Didot, 1894, pp. 7–8.

'Discours prononcé à l'inauguration de la statue de Joachim du Bellay à Ancenis, le dimanche 2 septembre 1894', Institut de France, Firmin-Didot, 1894, pp. 3–8.

'Discours de réception à l'Académie française, prononcé le 30 mai 1895', Lemerre, 1895.

'Daniel Vierge', preface to: Saint-Juirs, *Le Cabaret des trois vertus*, illustrations de Daniel Vierge, gravées par Clément Bellenger, Tallandier, 1895.

Letter published as preface to Philippe Dufour's *Poèmes légendaires*, Lemerre, 1897.

'Le Manuscrit des *Bucoliques*', *Revue des deux mondes*, 1 November 1905, pp. 146–67.

Preface to Comte Henry de la Vaulx, *Voyage en Patagonie*, Hachette, 1901, pp. v–xvi.

Translations of LES TROPHÉES

See Ibrovac, ii, pp. 579–83 for a list too long to reproduce here and also the two translations into Spanish mentioned above.

WRITINGS ON HEREDIA

Albalat, Antoine, 'José-Maria de Heredia et la poésie contemporaine', *La Nouvelle Revue*, 1 December 1894, pp. 523–47.

— 'Les "Samedis" de J.-M. de Heredia', *La Revue hebdomadaire*, 4 October 1919, pp. 34–70.

Bailey, John C., *The Claims of French Poetry*, London, Constable, 1907, pp. 283–313.

Barbey d'Aurevilly, Jules, *XIXe siècle* (2ème série): *Les Œuvres et les hommes: les poètes*, Lemerre, 1889.

Barracand, Léon, 'Souvenirs des lettres', *Revue de Paris*, 1 March 1914, pp. 183–96.

Barrès, Maurice, 'Discours prononcés dans la séance publique tenue par l'Académie française pour la réception de M. Maurice Barrès le jeudi 17 janvier 1907', Firmin-Didot, 1907.

Bayet, Charles, 'Obsèques', *In Memoriam*, Librarie Henri Leclerc, 1906, pp. 32–5.

Bordeaux, Henry, *La Vie et l'art. Ames modernes*, Perrin, 1895, pp. 131–161.

Bourget, Paul, 'Science et poésie: à propos des *Trophées*', *Essais de psychologie contemporaine*, Plon, 1926.

Brodel, Fernand, 'L'Elégie chez Heredia', *Mercure de France*, 15 August 1920, pp. 119–27.

Châtelain, U.-V., 'José-Maria de Heredia, sa vie et son milieu', *Cahiers des études littéraires françaises*, fascicule no. 2, undated.

Clouard, Henri, *Histoire de la littérature française du symbolisme à nos jours*, Michel, 1947.

Coppée, François, 'Réponse au discours de réception à l'Académie française de Heredia', Firmin-Didot, 1895.

Deschamps, Gaston, 'José-Maria de Heredia', *La Vie et les livres* (3ème série), Colin, 1896.

Faguet, Emile, 'José-Maria de Heredia', *Revue des poètes*, 10 October 1905.

Fontainas, André, 'José-Maria de Heredia', *Mercure de France*, 15 October 1905, pp. 481–7.

France, Anatole, *La Vie littéraire* (3ème série), Calmann-Lévy, 1893.

Fromm, Heinrich, *'Les Trophées' von José-Maria de Heredia*. Untersuchungen über den Aufbau, Reim und Stil. Inaugural-Dissertation zur Erlangung der Doktorwürde der Hohen Philosophischen Fakultät der Königlichen Universität Greifswald vorgelegt von Heinrich Fromm, Greifswald, 1913.

Galdemar, Ange, 'L'Œuvre posthume de Leconte de Lisle; conversation avec M. de Heredia', *Le Gaulois*, 19 May 1895.

Gaubert, Charles, *José-Maria de Heredia*, Rouen, L. Wolf, 1911.

Gide, André, *Journal 1889–1939*, Gallimard, 1951.

Goday, Armand, 'Le Poète des *Trophées* et l'Amérique', *Le Figaro*, *Supplément littéraire*, 17 October 1925.

Gourmont, Remy de, 'M. de Heredia et les poètes parnassiens', *Promenades littéraires* (2ème série), Mercure de France, 1913.

Grammont, Maurice, *Le Vers français. Ses moyens d'expression, son harmonie,* Delagrave, 1937.

Guignard, Jacques, 'A la Bibliothèque de l'Arsenal, le Centenaire de José-Maria de Heredia', *Sources—études, recherches, informations des Bibliothèques nationales de France,* Bibliothèque Nationale, 1943, p. 117.

Hamilo, Ludovic, *L'Evénement,* 8 March 1894.

Hanotaux, Gabriel, 'In Memoriam', pp. 5–15, and 'Heredia bibliophile et bibliothécaire', pp. 43–56, *In Memoriam,* Librairie Henri Leclerc, 1906.

Harms, Alvin, *José-Maria de Heredia,* Boston, U.S.A., Twayne Publishers, 1975.

Hébertot, Jacques *Le Sonnet, son évolution à travers les âges et les pays,* Bibliothèque indépendante, 1905.

Ibrovac, Miodrag, *José-Maria de Heredia: sa vie—son œuvre,* Les Presses françaises, 1923, vol. i. (Ibrovac i), vol. ii (Ibrovac ii).

—, *Les Sources des 'Trophées',* Les Presses françaises, 1923 (Ibrovac, *Sources*).

—, *Journal des débats,* 18 October 1925.

Jasinski, Max, *Histoire du sonnet en France,* Douai, Dalsheimer, 1903.

Kahn, Gustave, 'José-Maria de Heredia', *La Revue,* 15 October 1905.

Labarthe, André, *Poésies choisies de Stéphane Mallarmé et 'Les Trophées' de José-Maria de Heredia,* London, Barnard and Westwood, 1943.

Langevin, Eugène, 'José-Maria de Heredia—son œuvre poétique', *Le Correspondant,* 10 January 1907, pp. 53–82.

Lanson, Gustave, *Histoire de la littérature française,* Hachette, 1902.

Lavagne, J., 'José-Maria de Heredia', *Mémoires de la Société Dunkerquoise pour l'encouragement des sciences, des lettres et des arts,* 43ème volume, Dunkerque, 1906, pp. 107–21.

Le Cardonnel, Georges and Vellay, Charles, *La Littérature contemporaine. Opinions des écrivains de ce temps,* Mercure de France, 1905, pp. 283–8.

Lecomte, Georges, 'Heredia au Luxembourg', *La Renaissance politique, littéraire, artistique,* 29 December 1923.

Lemaître, Jules, 'José-Maria de Heredia', *Les Contemporains, études et portraits littéraires* (2ème série), Boivin, 1886, pp. 49–65.

Madeleine, Jacques, 'Chronologie des sonnets de José-Maria de Heredia', *Revue d'histoire littéraire de la France.* April-June 1912.

Mendès, Catulle, *La Légende du 'Parnasse contemporain',* Bruxelles, Brancart, 1884.

Morice, Charles, *La littérature de tout à l'heure,* Perrin, 1889, pp. 219–20.

Pellissier, Georges, 'José-Maria de Heredia', *Etudes de littérature contemporaine,* vol. i. Perrin, 1898, pp. 11–14.

Pichon, René, 'L'Antiquité romaine et la poésie française à l'époque parnassienne', *Revue des deux mondes,* 1 September 1911.

Poizat, Alfred, 'José-Maria de Heredia', *La Quinzaine*, 1 June 1895, pp. 281–92.

Prévost, Ernest, 'José-Maria de Heredia', *Le Figaro, Supplément littéraire*, 17 October 1925.

Régnier, Henri de, 'Discours de réception à l'Académie française, le 18 janvier 1912', Firmin-Didot, 1912, pp. 7–10.

Régnier, Henri de, *Portraits et souvenirs*, Mercure de France, 1913, pp. 41–2; 68–76; 77–84.

Richardson, Joanna, 'José-Maria de Heredia: An Unpublished Correspondence', *Modern Language Review*, 65 (January 1970), pp. 36–53.

Rosières, Raoul, 'M. J.-M. de Heredia', *La Revue bleue*, 25 May 1895, pp. 642–4.

Souriau, Maurice, *Histoire du Parnasse*, Spes, 1929.

Symons, Arthur, *The Symbolist Movement in Literature*, London, Constable, 1899, Introduction.

Szertics, Simone, *L'Héritage espagnol de José-Maria de Heredia*, Klincksieck, 1975.

Thauziès, Raoul, 'Etude sur les sources de J.-M. de Heredia dans les cinquante-sept premiers sonnets des *Trophées*,' *Revue des langues romanes*, 1910, tome liii, pp. 461–512 and 1911, tome lv, pp. 37–66.

Vellay, Charles, See Le Cardonnel.

Verlaine, Paul, *Les Hommes d'aujourd'hui*, Gallimard, Bibliothèque de la Pléiade, 1972, pp. 866–7.

Vianey, Joseph, 'Les Sonnets grecs de Heredia', *Revue des cours et conférences*, 29 June (pp. 721–35) and 6 July (pp. 769–84) 1911.

Vogüé, vicomte Melchior de, 'Obsèques', *In Memoriam*, Librairie Henri Leclerc, 1906, pp. 26–32.

—, 'Discours prononcés dans la séance publique tenue par l'Académie française pour la réception de M. Maurice Barrès, le 18 janvier 1907', Firmin-Didot, 1907.

Zilliacus, Emile, 'José-Maria de Heredia et *l'Anthologie grecque*', *Revue d'histoire littéraire de la France*, April-June, 1910.

WORKS BY OTHERS

Asselineau, Charles, *Histoire du sonnet*, first published in 1856, reprinted in *Le Livre des sonnets*, Lemerre, 1874, pp. v-xxxv.

Chizeray-Cuny, Henriette de, *Marie de Régnier (Gérard d'Houville): propos et souvenirs*, Les Presses de l'office mécanographique à Paris, 1969.

Díaz del Castillo, Bernal, *The True History of the Conquest of New Spain by Bernal Díaz del Castillo, One of its Conquerors*. From the only exact copy made of the Original Manuscript. Edited and Published in Mexico by Genaro Garcia. Translated into English, with Introduction and

Notes, by Alfred Percival Maudslay, M.A., Hon. Professor of Archaeology, National Museum, Mexico. Published by the Hakluyt Society, 4 volumes, 1908–16.

Díaz del Castillo, Bernal, *Historia Verdadera de la Conquista de la Nueva España*, Introducción y notas de Joaquín Ramirez Cabañas, segunda edición, Editorial Porrua, S.A., Mexico, 1962.

Díaz del Castillo, Bernal, *The Conquest of New Spain*, translated with an introduction by J. M. Cohen, Penguin Books, 1963.

Erauso, Catalina de, *Historia de la Monja Alferez Doña Catalina de Erauso, escrita por elle misma*. Ilustrada con notas y documentos por D. Joaquín de Ferrer, Paris, Didot, 1829.

Erauso, Catalina de, *The Nun Ensign*. Translated from the Spanish with an introduction and notes by James FitzMaurice-Kelly. Illustrated by Daniel Vierge. London. T. Fisher Unwin. 1908.

Fairlie, Alison, *Leconte de Lisle's Poems on the Barbarian Races*, O.U.P., 1947.

Gérard d'Houville (Marie de Régnier), *Poésies*, Grasset, 1931.

Hytier, Jean, 'L'Esthétique valéryenne du sonnet', *Australian Journal of French Studies*, vi (1969), pp. 326–36.

Kesteloot, Lilyan, *Les Ecrivains noirs de langue française: naissance d'une littérature*, Editions de l'Institut de Sociologie, Université libre de Bruxelles, 1971.

Léautaud, Paul, *Journal littéraire*, Mercure de France, vol. ii, 1915 and vol. xii, 1962.

Prescott, W. H., *Histoire de la conquête du Pérou, précédée d'un tableau de la civilisation des Incas*, traduite de l'anglais par H. Poret, Firmin-Didot, 1861–3, three vols.

Proust, Marcel, *Contre Sainte-Beuve*, Gallimard, Bibliothèque de la Pléiade, 1961, pp. 211–312.

Valéry, Paul, 'Le Premier Article de Paul Valéry', *Dossiers*, Janin, 1946, pp. 13–20.

Valéry, Paul, 'Autres Rhumbs', *Œuvres*, Gallimard, Bibliothèque de la Pléiade, tome ii, 1960.

Valéry, Paul, *Cahiers Paul Valéry: I. Poétique et poésie*, Gallimard, 1975.

INDEX